Mysteries of the Glory Unveiled
Study Guide and Journal

Mysteries of the Glory Unveiled Study Guide and Journal

A New Wave of Signs and Wonders

DAVID HERZOG

DESTINY IMAGE® PUBLISHERS, INC.
P.O. Box 310, Shippensburg, PA 17257-0310

*"Speaking to the Purposes of God for this Generation
and for the Generations to Come."*

This book and all other Destiny Image, Revival Press, Mercy Place, Fresh Bread, Destiny Image Fiction, and Treasure House books are available at Christian bookstores and distributors worldwide.

For a U.S. bookstore nearest you, call 1-800-722-6774.
For more information on foreign distributors, call 717-532-3040.
Reach us on the Internet: www.destinyimage.com.

ISBN 10: 0-7684-2639-1
ISBN 13: 978-0-7684-2639-7

For Worldwide Distribution, Printed in the U.S.A.

1 2 3 4 5 6 7 8 9 10 11 / 09 08

Contents

DAY 1

Signs and Wonders

" 'THE SILVER IS MINE, AND THE GOLD IS MINE,' SAYS THE LORD OF HOSTS. 'THE GLORY OF THIS LATTER TEMPLE SHALL BE GREATER THAN THE FORMER,' SAYS THE LORD OF HOSTS" (HAGGAI 2:8-9A).

The revival in Paris started when we conducted a 40-day prayer and fasting chain. This brought a spirit of repentance upon the Christians and caused them to come forward and publicly seek forgiveness. Many testified that their secret sins had left them with terrible guilt and shame. Now they were free.

Articles used for sin—pornography, drugs and drug paraphernalia, and various items used in witchcraft—were thrown on the altar each night and forsaken. God had spoken to us that believers should not only ask God to forgive their sin, but should allow Him to break the power of sin in their lives. And this He did.

When the power of sin began to break off of the church, this loosed a wave of sinners to come to the feet of Jesus and be saved. There seemed to be a magnet drawing people in night after night. Those who were saved included atheists, witches, gang members, drug addicts, nominal Christians and people of other religions. Young and old alike received Jesus as Savior.

There were many healings and miracles demonstrated publicly each night in these meetings. Deaf ears opened. Paralyzed people were healed. Many with incurable diseases and serious cancers were healed. Every type of miracle was seen in Paris during those days.

QUESTIONS

1. Have you ever been part of a revival meeting or a season of revival? What demonstrations of the presence and power of God are evidenced in a revival? How do you know whether these demonstrations are real or not?

2. In the excerpt above, what is the progression of spiritual events? (First, there was prayer and fasting. Second, etc.) What does this progression tell you about God's priorities?

3. Do you have a desire to see God's revival come to you personally? What price needs to be paid for a visitation of God's glory upon your life? What should you do next?

4. Why does forgiveness first come to the house of God before going out into the other parts of society? If the Church does not repent and receive forgiveness, is there no hope for revival? Why does God use corporate repentance instead of a few repentant individuals within the church?

5. How is the power of sin over the life of a sinner broken? How can we be sure that the experience is real and lasting for those who participate in these corporate times of repentance? How should the Church embrace those people who are drawn to revival from outside the walls of our churches? What specific things should we do to establish them in their new walk?

*"Many testified that their secret sins
had left them with terrible guilt and shame."*

What secret sin is God asking you
to confess and repent before Him?

Do you think these sins could be
holding the Church back from seeing revival?

A Revival of Signs and Wonders

"Go and tell John the things you have seen and heard: that the blind see, the lame walk, the lepers are cleansed, the deaf hear, the dead are raised, the poor have the gospel preached to them. And blessed is he who is not offended because of Me" (Luke 7:22-23).

"Blessed is he who is not offended." It is easy to miss a new move of God or to be "offended" as each new move comes. It happens largely because revival takes on a different form each time it comes. Each wave is a little different. Many people, for instance, are still looking for the restoration of the 1950 Revival. While this new move of God will have many of the characteristics of that one, it will also have many new elements.

God seems to package revival in such a way as to attract only those who are desperate for Him. The hungry are somehow able to see what God is doing through strange new circumstances, rather than judging by outward appearances. When people are expecting God to bring revival in the way they have known in the past—and it comes in a totally different form instead—it seems easy for them to reject it. The sad thing is that they just keep waiting for something else to come along.

We must be careful. That which we reject may very well be the beginning of what we have been waiting and praying for. The people of Israel were waiting for their Messiah, but when He showed up in a most unexpected way, the religious community rejected Him. Despite the great things that Jesus did, the Jewish leaders of His day somehow could not recognize that He was what they had prayed and hoped for for so long.

QUESTIONS

1. Have you ever been offended or do you know someone who has been offended by Jesus? In your experience, does this offense come from opinion, unbelief, or lack of understanding? Do you think there is any way that we can help people who are offended by Christ?

2. Why do you think people want the experiences associated with revival to be identical for each successive revival? Why does change tend to make people suspicious? What experiences do you question as to their validity?

3. Why do you think God chooses to package revival so that it attracts only those who are desperate for Him? How does their desperation help them see past the outward experiences of the revival that may seem unusual?

4. Think about the Pharisees and Sadducees during Jesus' ministry. Was their acceptance or rejection of him based on their own worldview of what was "supposed to happen"? How has your worldview shaped what you accept or reject?

5. The common people of Israel rejected Jesus as well. What kept them from seeing the truth? Have you ever rejected the truth of something God has done, only to find out later you should have not only accepted it, but participated in it?

MEDITATION

*"...the Jewish people of His (Jesus') day
somehow could not recognize that He was
what they had prayed and hoped for for so long."*

What will keep you from missing the next
wave of revival that God brings to the world?

Even though you pray or hope for revival,
what may keep you from recognizing it?

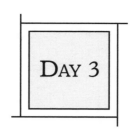

DAY 3

Why the Gold?

" **A**ND HIS GLORY WILL BE SEEN UPON YOU" (ISAIAH 60:2B).

When I shifted out of neutral and put myself strongly on the Lord's side, suddenly the gold was appearing everywhere I ministered. Many people have asked what all this means, and it is a legitimate question. Our second child, Shannon Glory, was born at the beginning of all of this manifestation, and Debbie Kendrick prophesied that she would be "a sign and a wonder." When Shannon was born, there was gold dust all over her face, and she continues to have this manifestation to this day.

Moses had a visible manifestation of the glory when his face shone. Many others in the Bible experienced the same thing. The Bible foretold that great signs and wonders would be seen in the last days, and this is one of them. Since God is still a Creator, He is still in the business of creating new things. Each new move of His Spirit has its own mark upon it.

The gold dust is not an end in itself. It is only a sign of what is to come. When the gold appears, it is an indication that the atmosphere in a meeting is charged for miracles, and anything can happen. This is the same anointing in which Elijah and Jesus operated. They performed miracles, signs and wonders, raised the dead, and saw miraculous provision. By sending this unusual manifestation into our midst, God is saying to us that we can expect to see the same things.

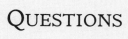

QUESTIONS

1. How is gold one of the best representations of God's glory? How does its association with being a "precious" metal bring intensity to the experience of the glory of God?

2. Do you see a spiritual purpose for the appearances of gold during seasons of revival? Do you see any scriptural references to gold that can give a clue to the value of gold in God's eyes?

3. When Moses had a visible manifestation of the glory of God, how did the people react? Why did they have trouble enduring his appearance? What spiritual significance was the veil that they made him wear? Do we ever "veil" manifestations of God's presence because we cannot endure them?

4. How do you think the appearances of gold are signs of what is to come? Do you think these experiences help people receive miracles and blessings that they would not have otherwise?

5. How did God use the unusual manifestations of His glory within the signs and wonders that Elijah performed? Within Jesus' miracles? Why should we expect more unusual manifestations in the future?

MEDITATION

"I am convinced that in the days ahead we will see many of the miracles that accompanied Jesus while He was on the Earth, and the signs and wonders we see will also be too many and too diverse to be recorded."

Is this statement difficult or easy for you to embrace and believe?

Why will the diversity and volume of signs and wonders be necessary?

DAY 4

A Harvest-Producing Rain

"Ask the Lord for rain in the time of the latter rain. The Lord will make flashing clouds; He will give them showers of rain, grass in the field for everyone" (Zechariah 10:1).

Most of us who are attuned to God's Spirit have come to believe that a great harvest of souls is on His immediate agenda, and we have become very interested in the subject of harvest. Throughout history, great outpourings of the Holy Spirit have been accompanied by great harvests of souls.

The first such outpouring took place, of course, on the Day of Pentecost. That day, people were refreshed, revived, empowered and filled with joy. Soon thereafter, three thousand souls were saved, and this great harvest of souls continued in the fledgling Church on a daily basis.

As the harvest grew ever larger, some in the affected areas became alarmed, and persecution broke out against the Church. This resulted in the disciples needing another wave of empowerment, so that they could remain faithful to God. In response, He sent them another refreshing rain:

> *And when they had prayed, the place where they were assembled together was shaken; and they were all filled with the Holy Spirit, and they spoke the word of God with boldness* (Acts 4:31).

Each time the Holy Spirit is poured out over a thirsty land, it produces a harvest. "And believers were *the more added to the Lord,* multitudes both of men and women" (Acts 5:14 KJV). "Then the churches throughout all Judea, Galilee, and Samaria had peace and were edified. And walking in the fear of the Lord and in the comfort of the Holy Spirit, *they were multiplied*" (Acts 9:31).

QUESTIONS

1. If the harvest of souls is a high priority on God's agenda, why do you think we don't see more people saved? How have historic revivals gathered many souls in a short period of time? How can the Church use this knowledge for today's harvest?

2. The people who experienced the Day of Pentecost "were refreshed, revived, empowered and filled with joy." How is this a miracle in and of itself? How do you think this prepared the people for what happened next? Do we need this same kind of preparation?

3. If your local church added 3,000 people in one day, what problems would it face? How do you think the disciples handled the spiritual demands of their massive new flock? What do you think sustained the disciples? What sustained the new converts?

4. What ingredients do you think the Jerusalem church had as they met daily and added new converts daily? Do you think these ingredients are important to duplicate in today's local churches? What part should you play in bringing the harvest to your church?

5. Why did God allow persecution to besiege the early church? As the Christians were persecuted, what was required so that they could sustain their focus and priority of gathering souls? Do you think today's churches perceive that God uses persecution as a means to a kingdom end? What should churches seek in order to not only go through the persecution but to be able to continue in their primary work of the kingdom?

MEDITATION

"Each time the Holy Spirit is poured out over a thirsty land, it produces a harvest."

Is your nation thirsty?

Is your church thirsty?

Are you thirsty?

What is the difference between being thirsty and being needy?

DAY 5

The Golden Glory

"ARISE, SHINE; FOR YOUR LIGHT HAS COME! AND THE GLORY OF THE LORD IS RISEN UPON YOU" (ISAIAH 60:1).

Gold is the color of harvest. Wheat especially, when it is ready to collect, has a beautiful golden color. As God pours out His Spirit in this unusual way, the golden glory is attracting people in record numbers. This has proven to be a most powerful tool for evangelism. People are curious, and this manifestation draws the curious.

But there are other reasons. The gold is a visible sign that the glory of God has returned to His people, and that glory draws men and women. Men who have "sinned, and come short of the glory of God" (Romans 3:23 KJV) are drawn to it when they hear that it has appeared. When they see it manifested, they are drawn to repentance and are saved.

When the glory of God is seen upon us, people are attracted to it like metal to a magnet. This makes it easy for us to bring in the harvest. It is just as God showed Isaiah it would be:

> *The Gentiles shall come to your light,*
> *And kings to the brightness of your rising.*
> *"Lift up your eyes all around, and see;*
> *They all gather together, they come to you;*
> *Your sons shall come from afar,*
> *And your daughters shall be nursed at your side"*
> (Isaiah 60:3-4).

The manifestation of the glory of God leads to a harvest of souls, the rain of the Spirit producing a bumper crop.

QUESTIONS

1. In your opinion, is there a correlation between the gold color of harvest and the manifestation of gold in recent outpourings of God? How tied together are revivals and harvests of souls?

2. When people are curious about the appearances of gold at revivals, do you think God uses their curiosity to open them to the Gospel or does it fan disbelief? How does your curiosity work? Do you think curiosity opens you to new experiences or does your spirit and soul close at new experiences because of fear or unbelief?

3. How does the appearance of gold represent purity? How is it a visible sign of God's glory? How can you prepare your heart for revival by dealing with the area of personal purity? In what ways are you to reflect God's glory?

4. Has God's glory ever "risen upon you" so that people have been drawn to you and received ministry? How does your light become a beacon to people through your gifts and your character?

5. Are you prepared to harvest souls if they are drawn to you? Do you have the basics of Christianity ready on your tongue and in your mind so that you can share the tenets of salvation easily and joyfully with others? Is there any other way you should prepare?

*"The Gentiles shall come to your light, and
kings to the brightness of your rising" (Isaiah 60:3).*

How bright is your light?

Would it surprise you if you drew people from a vast
array of religious and cultural backgrounds (Gentiles)?

Would you be shocked if your light
drew people of influence (kings)?

Can you believe that you will have
a vast impact for the kingdom?

Day 6

The Elijah Anointing

"BEHOLD, I WILL SEND YOU ELIJAH THE PROPHET BEFORE THE COMING OF THE GREAT AND DREADFUL DAY OF THE LORD" (MALACHI 4:5).

TODAY'S DEVOTION

God has promised that the Church would return to the spirit of Elijah, and we must be able to discern the signs of the times, as Elijah did.

We have been taught for many years the importance of weeping for souls, of having a burden for nations and cities, and this typified the ministry of Jeremiah. Jesus also had great compassion for souls and wept for the city of Jerusalem.

We have had a resurgence of the spirit of holiness and repentance, most recently during the Pensacola Revival (which is still continuing), and this typified the mantle of John the Baptist. Jesus preached repentance, just as John did. Some even thought that He was John risen from the dead.

Elijah confronted and challenged the sorcerers of his day with greater miracles, signs and wonders, causing great revival. He raised the dead, healed the sick, had authority over nature, and performed many unusual miracles—beginning and ending with provisional miracles.

Jesus came in that same anointing. He raised Lazarus from the dead, multiplied bread and turned water into wine, healed the sick, and challenged every power and authority of His day.

The apostles continued in Jesus' footsteps, and the same glory that empowered them is at work again today. The Elijah anointing is now coming upon the Church.

QUESTIONS

1. In your opinion, what is the "spirit of Elijah"? How did Elijah discern the signs of the times? How are we able to discern these signs?

2. Have you been a part of the type of ministry that resembles Jeremiah's? What are the ways Jeremiah demonstrated his burden for people and cities? How did Jesus show His compassion for souls?

3. Compare and contrast the ministries of Elijah and Jesus. Do you participate in any activities of ministry that they did? In what areas would you like to grow so that your ministry resembles theirs more?

4. How do signs and wonders become objects of confrontation for those who doubt or for people who do not believe in God? How did Elijah's authority both confront people and display God's miracle power? How can your authority do the same?

5. Both Elijah and Jesus performed provisional miracles. What are some of these miracles with which you are familiar? How do the types of miracles that meet people's needs open them up for the Gospel?

MEDITATION

"The apostles continued in Jesus' footsteps, and the same glory that empowered them is at work again today."

Are you currently demonstrating
that kind of glory in your life?

Do you receive the anointing of Elijah with the
responsibility that comes with that anointing?

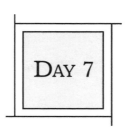

The Key to Creative Miracles

IN THE BEGINNING GOD CREATED THE HEAVENS AND THE EARTH. THE EARTH WAS FORMLESS AND EMPTY, AND DARKNESS COVERED THE DEEP WATERS. AND THE SPIRIT OF GOD WAS HOVERING OVER THE SURFACE OF THE WATERS. THEN GOD SAID, "LET THERE BE LIGHT," AND THERE WAS LIGHT (GENESIS 1:1-3 NLT).

"The Spirit of God was hovering over its surface." This is the most important secret we can learn about operating in creative miracles. When the presence of God, His glory, begins to hover over a place or a person, the power and potential for creative miracles is present. Releasing this working of creative miracles must be done while the Spirit is hovering in this way. It is an act so simple that most of us miss it.

While the Spirit hovered, God the Father spoke. He said, "Let there be light," and when He said that, light was created. Everything that God created was created in this same way. God spoke it into being. Every living thing was spoken into being by God.

As the crowning glory of His creation, God made us. We are created in His image and were meant to be His representatives on the Earth. We can now speak on His behalf. We can declare what He shows us He wants to do.

When the presence of God is hovering over you in a given place, and you hear His voice saying something like "cancers are dissolving" or "limbs are growing back," you must do what God did. You must speak those words out. Learn to do it spontaneously as He is saying it, and when you do, creative miracles will begin to manifest themselves.

QUESTIONS

1. Have you ever felt the Spirit of God hovering over a place where you were worshiping? What did the presence of God feel like? What made the experience unforgettable? How hard is it for our fast-paced society to take the time for the Holy Spirit to hover in our meetings? How long is your attention span in the midst of corporate worship?

2. What is the connection between the Spirit hovering and the Father speaking? How does God's Word come into play when the presence of God is felt during our services or meetings? Has God spoken to you individually during a time of worship, because you were listening and clearing your thoughts of everything but Him?

3. How do you know that you are the crowning glory of God's creation? Is it by outward beauty? Do talents or gifts have anything to do with it? Is it because you are intelligent or have a great personality? How does being created in His image make the difference between us and the rest of creation?

4. Since you are made in the image of God Almighty, you are His emissary and ambassador. You can speak on His behalf and do what He would do. How can you remain in tune with God so that you are constantly, ceaselessly hearing, speaking and doing His will?

5. Have you heard words of knowledge in your heart during corporate worship? Is it easy for you to speak out words of knowledge if you receive them? Have you experienced speaking something the Lord gave to you and watching a miracle take place? What glory do you get from giving this kind of message? Where does the glory begin? As the glory passes through you, where does the glory end up going?

MEDITATION

"If we stop to analyze what we are hearing in such moments (out of fear), and we hesitate or procrastinate, the moment can be lost. The quicker we act on what God is saying, the more easily and dramatically the creative miracle will occur. This is especially true when God is saying something that seems absolutely impossible or beyond our faith level."

Did you ever have this type of experience?

Have you been afraid of the impossibility of what God has said?

How can we turn from unbelief to a position of faith?

Day 8

Going Beyond the Limitations of Our Own Faith

"**M**Y SHEEP HEAR MY VOICE, AND I KNOW THEM, AND THEY FOLLOW ME" (JOHN 10:27).

The things God calls us to do in the realm of creative miracles are always beyond our faith level. So, though we sense that the glory of God is hovering over us, it is easy to let our reasoning get in the way of action. It is no longer a question of having enough faith to do the miracle. The only question is: who is speaking? We might also ask: will we rise to the challenge?

When we become convinced that the Creator Himself is speaking through us, we know that all we must do is obey. We use our faith to tap into God's glory, but once we do, acting creatively demands that we only listen and obey. The work to be done is the work of the Creator. It is His glory that does the work, not anything that we can do ourselves.

When we learn to speak before we have had the chance to analyze the impossibility of what we are saying, the miracle is already done. Entering the creative realm, then, is as simple as hearing the Lord and following His instructions.

Scientists have come to use the speed at which light travels as a scientific measurement. But light is only symbolic of God's glory, and the speed of light is but a shadow of the speed of God's glory. Miracles are created at the speed of glory, for in glory there is no limit of time as we know it.

1. Why do you think God calls us to go beyond our faith level when it comes to miracles? How does He use the experience of miracles to pull us into a new level of faith? Do you find it hard to rise to the challenge of faith in terms of signs and wonders? How can Christians embrace these events with greater expectancy and faith?

2. How do you know if God is speaking to you or not? What inner witness do you have? How can you prove that what you hear is truth? Is it easy to convince you that it is God speaking, or do doubts remain?

3. When you were a toddler, what were the first principles of behavior that your parents or guardians taught you? Why do you think humans seem to take a lifetime to learn how to listen and obey? How can something so simple be the key to operating in the creative move of His Spirit to perform signs and wonders?

4. How does someone move "out of the way" and let God do the work of His glory? What place does humility have in the apportionment of seeing miracles take place through you? What place does servanthood have?

5. When we think in earthly terms, we are bound by earth. Thinking in kingdom terms frees us to do kingdom work. In what areas of kingdom work are you bound by an earthly worldview? Where does God need to free you before you can free others?

MEDITATION

"Miracles are created at the speed of glory, for in glory there is no limit of time as we know it."

What does this statement mean to you?

Does this explain immediate miracles and those that take time to develop?

How does this concept free us from boxing God into our perimeters of understanding?

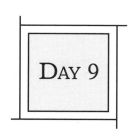

DAY 9

Why Miracles Sometimes Don't Happen

" AND GREAT MULTITUDES FOLLOWED HIM, AND **HE HEALED THEM ALL**" (MATTHEW 12:15).

Sometimes we use our faith to speak things we would like to see happen, or we lay hands on people we would like to see healed or delivered. If we were to be honest, we would have to say that our ministry results sometimes seem to be hit-and-miss. We do not receive total victory for every person we pray for. This leads us to wonder how Jesus achieved instant and total results when He ministered to the people of His day.

What was the secret of the Lord's one hundred percent instant results? He said: "...as the Father gave me commandment, even so I do"(John 14:31 KJV).

Tapping into the glory requires doing what the Father commands. It is His command that is powerful, not ours. It is His command that is creative, not ours. When God speaks and we simply say or do what He is saying or doing, spontaneous miracles occur.

Someone might argue that God has already given us the privilege of laying hands on the sick and seeing miracles of healing performed. Why do we need something more? We can act on our faith, lay hands on the sick, and expect them to recover. These are good methods of ministry, but we should not be limited by them. If we use our faith as a tool to tap into the glory, not as an end in itself, we can rise to higher levels of God's presence and power.

1. Have you ever felt that your ministry prayers have been hit-and-miss in terms of visible results? How did these results either anchor your faith or make it waver toward your ability to be a channel for God's miracles?

2. Think through the healing and deliverance ministry of Jesus. He healed each one and saw the results. What processes (laying on of hands, etc.) did He use? How did he know which process to use? How can we know what to do during healing and deliverance ministry?

3. "Tapping into the glory requires doing what the Father commands." How does this reflect the simple process of hearing and obeying? Why do you think we tend not to hear what God wants us to do?

4. Explain how miracles are merely God's creativity at work. As Creator, why does He own all miracles, great and small? What part do we play in the process?

5. What processes are available to us as we learn to hear and obey God? Are we to use only one process in praying for the sick? How does our faith bring us to the point of hearing? How does faith connect us to the courage to obey?

MEDITATION

"We can work hard and stay in the faith and see good results, or we can use our faith to rise into the glory realm. Once there, as we do and say what we see God doing and saying, there will be immediate and lasting results."

Have you experienced the
truth of these statements?

How do you reach the glory realm?

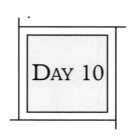

DAY 10

The Faith Realm Versus the Glory Realm

"THEREFORE, LEAVING THE DISCUSSION OF THE ELEMENTARY PRINCIPLES OF CHRIST, LET US GO ON TO PERFECTION, NOT LAYING AGAIN THE FOUNDATION OF REPENTANCE FROM DEAD WORKS AND OF FAITH TOWARD GOD, OF THE DOCTRINE OF BAPTISMS, OF LAYING ON OF HANDS, OF RESURRECTION OF THE DEAD, AND OF ETERNAL JUDGMENT" (HEBREWS 6:1–2).

Heaven is filled with God's glory. There will be no sickness there. Therefore when we speak a word of healing or miracles in the glory, there are instant results. Wonderful things can be done in the faith realm, but greater things can be done in the glory realm.

I have seen cancers fall off, deaf ears pop open, bald heads grow hair, and a multitude of other miracles happen simply by speaking what I heard at that moment. I have seen teeth filled and crowned with gold over and over again, as I heard God say it, and I began to declare it.

True, I have also seen similar results with the laying on of hands, but I have noticed that many more people are healed by the spoken word of God than through the laying on of hands. And it happens much more quickly.

When we are in meetings with thousands of people, it is physically difficult to lay hands on everyone. However, we can speak a word that we hear from Heaven, and instantly hundreds can be healed at one time.

Laying hands on everyone is an acceptable method for bringing healing, but it is very tiring to lay hands on everyone when there is a large group. We must not allow our limitations to prevent us from having God's best. Tap into all His resources and experience His miracles.

QUESTIONS

1. When we speak a word of healing or miracles in the glory, how does this reveal Heaven? How does this process bring a little Heaven to the earth?

2. Think through your experiences as you have observed people laying hands on the sick and the results that were produced and the times people spoke words of knowledge over people. Compare them. If you could estimate a percentage of spontaneous miracles, what would it be in either situation? Can you explain why there is a difference, if any?

3. Tapping into God's glory for miracles is practical as well as supernatural. Can you explain how this is true? Have you seen a great number of people healed or delivered at the same time due to a spoken word from Heaven?

4. How do we tend to limit ourselves from God's best in terms of receiving our blessings? How do we tend to limit Him within the scope of our ministry? What can we do to change so that the limits are taken off and we are able to do even greater works than Jesus?

5. Look at the Hebrews passage above. What six tenets are the foundation principles that we must understand? Why do you think "laying on of hands" is an elementary and not an advanced principle of Christ? How must our thinking change in this regard?

MEDITATION

"Our spontaneous obedience to what God is telling us to do or say determines whether or not miracles will actually be manifested."

Why does this obedience
need to be "spontaneous"?

What does spontaneous
obedience reveal about our faith?

What does spontaneous obedience
show about our willingness to obey?

Day 11

Miracles Manifest the Glory

"JESUS SAID TO HER, 'DID I NOT SAY TO YOU THAT IF YOU WOULD BELIEVE YOU WOULD SEE THE GLORY OF GOD?'" (JOHN 11:40)

TODAY'S DEVOTION

When Jesus raised Lazarus by the spoken word, He did it to manifest the glory that was already present: "He said, 'This sickness is not unto death, but for the glory of God, that the Son of God may be glorified through it'" (John 11:4).

Jesus was able to say that Lazarus was not dead, because He heard His Father say it. Then He walked into the frame provided and thus completed the picture by speaking life into the dead man.

It is one thing to feel the presence and glory of God in a meeting, and it is quite another thing to have that glory manifested. Miracles make the glory real to us. The glory is a cloud that hovers over our lives, and in the glory cloud, there is the potential for miracles, revival and harvest.

When the glory cloud hovers over us, a sense of expectancy fills us, for we know that anything is possible. Far too many people rest in the fact that the cloud is present, and are content to wait for its manifestation—in rain, revival, miracles or harvest.

In order for a natural cloud to produce rain, it is not enough that it be seen and felt. There must be an atmospheric pressure in the air to cause rain. This is a scientific fact in the natural world, and it is true in the spiritual world as well. The pressure needed is our continued hunger and desperate desire to see the glory.

QUESTIONS

1. "Miracles are a manifestation of the glory of God." Can you explain this statement in light of your experiences thus far?

2. The situation with Lazarus and his family was a "frame provided" for the manifest presence of God to be seen through a miracle. How well do you read the situations you face to see them as "frames provided" for God's miraculous nature to be made visible?

3. Have you ever felt the cloud of glory hover over you in a meeting so that your heart was filled with expectancy and joy? Why do we tend to see this cloud as an end in itself and not the atmosphere for further glory to be revealed?

4. When Christians are content to have just enough presence of God to make them feel good, what does that indicate about their faith walk? How does lethargy play into the absence of miracles?

5. What kind of spiritual pressure is needed to produce the glory that results in miracles? What do you think this spiritual pressure looks like or feels like? What responsibility do you have to press through as an individual within a corporate meeting until spontaneous miracles occur?

MEDITATION

"Like Moses, we must cry out to
God until the manifestation comes."

Think back through the instances where
Moses cried out to God and there was
a spontaneous miracle. How desperate
was Moses for the manifestation of God?

Do you cry out to God until the
manifestation of His presence comes?

DAY 12

Today Is the Day

"FOR ALL WHO WERE POSSESSORS...BROUGHT THE PROCEEDS OF THE THINGS THAT WERE SOLD, AND LAID THEM AT THE APOSTLES' FEET; AND THEY DISTRIBUTED TO EACH AS ANYONE HAD NEED" (ACTS 4:34-35).

TODAY'S DEVOTION

The believers of the first century sometimes became desperate in their search for God. At times, their desperation was driven by serious persecution and they prayed fervently: "Now, Lord, look on their threats, and grant to Your servants that with all boldness they may speak Your word, by stretching out Your hand to heal, and that signs and wonders may be done through the name of Your holy Servant Jesus" (Acts 4:29-30).

The disciples were asking God to do healings, signs and wonders because they believed that such signs and wonders would be the most powerful means of validating or confirming what they were preaching.

Each new move of the Spirit has a new outpouring of power that comes with it and new manifestations and new truths that are revealed. The outpouring of Pentecost was different from the outpouring in the fourth chapter of Acts: "And when they had prayed, the place where they were assembled together was shaken; and they were all filled with the Holy Spirit, and they spoke the word of God with boldness" (Acts 4:31).

We go "from glory to glory," and each new glory has a new manifestation. If the apostles had insisted that the experience of the initial Day of Pentecost outpouring was the only pattern for revival, they never would have progressed. When a move of God's Spirit stops moving, it is no longer a move, and it becomes part of history.

QUESTIONS

1. How desperate are you in your search for God? What types of circumstances or events aid in your desperation? What do you do to find God during times of desperation?

2. Think through times when persecution came upon the Church of the New Testament. What did they do to seek God and bring His power to bear on their behalf? How was it released? Does the Church need persecution in order to become so desperate that they seek God with all their heart?

3. How do signs and wonders validate what we say? Do you think the lack of signs and wonders today has hurt our testimony? Just as Pharaoh's magicians explained Moses' signs away, just as the Pharisees tried to hide the miracles of Jesus, can we expect people today to react negatively to the sensational nature of signs and wonders that the Church will operate in today?

4. How bold are you to proclaim the Word of the Lord? Is it easier in certain settings than others? Do you find sharing God's Word easier with some people than others? Does your boldness wane or increase when under persecution?

5. What do you think it means when we go "from glory to glory"? How do manifestations change as each time of glory occurs? Why should we not compare current glory to glory in the past?

MEDITATION

"When God moves in a new way, we cannot always compare it to past moves to see if it is of Him. He does new things, so if we are to be pioneers in bringing something new, we must allow God to do things that bypass our current experience."

Do you have the heart of a pioneer?

How can tell if you do or don't have an adventuring spirit?

How does God use pioneers to enter in His new manifestations of glory?

DAY 13

The New Sign

"NOW THE MULTITUDE OF THOSE WHO BELIEVED WERE OF ONE HEART AND ONE SOUL; NEITHER DID ANYONE SAY THAT ANY OF THE THINGS HE POSSESSED WAS HIS OWN, BUT THEY HAD ALL THINGS IN COMMON" (ACTS 4:32).

As the disciples gave to one another and the apostles, the power of God was turned on in their lives. Suddenly, they "had all things in common." This refers to more than a physical sharing. They all had the same anointing and the same glory.

The men who had accompanied Jesus during His time on the Earth were not the only blessed ones. All of the believers were blessed equally. This resulted in "great power" within the Church: "And with great power the apostles gave witness to the resurrection of the Lord Jesus. And great grace was upon them all" (Acts 4:33).

With the spirit of spontaneous giving came an explosion of "great power." When we sow into the life of a minister or the life of a ministry that has the glory, we get part of that glory back upon our own lives and ministries.

"Great grace was upon them all." What a wonderful testimony! The great grace that the disciples of Jesus experienced after Calvary became common to all believers. I have found that a grace for signs, wonders and miracles comes corporately when the spirit of spontaneous giving erupts in a meeting.

When the early believers began laying money at the feet of the apostles, they were simply responding to the glory of God that rested on the apostles. There is a spiritual principle here: you reap what you sow.

Sowing a gift to empower a ministry to do more is a way of sowing to a level of grace on that minister's life and having a measure of it operate in your own life.

1. How do you see the power of God connected to our acts of giving? Explain what types of things the early Church had "in common" other than material things. Should we expect to see an anointing rest on everyone within a local congregation as God manifests His glory on it?

2. What is "great grace"? How do you think this grace was manifested on all of the people in the early Church? Would this have created a unifying bond that was beyond what any human bond could have been?

3. As you think about how Elisha served Elijah, would Elijah's grace have rested on Elisha even before the mantle was given to him? In what ways would Elisha have not only experienced great grace but had opportunity to learn how to use it?

4. How does the principle of sowing and glory work in your opinion? Why does God require a response to the anointing before we see manifestations in signs and wonders?

5. How would you know if God was asking you to give to a ministry in order to sow a seed of faith? How hard would it be to obey? Is He asking you to do so now?

MEDITATION

*"When you give, you help magnify the ability
of a ministry, enabling it to do more and reach
farther. As a result, you take part of the grace
that is upon that ministry. This is not the only way
to accomplish it, but it is a key that God is revealing
to us today that will unlock a new level of glory."*

Has God asked you to sow into a ministry?

Can you recognize the grace
that accompanies that ministry?

Should you expect to receive that same grace on
your own life as a result of your obedience to sow?

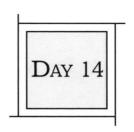

DAY 14

Spontaneous Giving Releases Resurrection Power

"And with great power the apostles gave witness to the **RESURRECTION** of the Lord Jesus" (Acts 4:33a).

TODAY'S DEVOTION

In Montreal, the gold dust began to fall after a spirit of spontaneous giving had broken out in the meeting while I was still preaching. Luigi, an evangelist, handed me an offering. He told me that he needed to sow into the glory that was working in my life.

The Lord told me to accept the money and to prophesy over Luigi. I prophesied that he would do greater things, and that very soon he would raise the dead. Within a week he had his opportunity.

He was in the emergency room waiting to have minor surgery, when someone wheeled in a dead woman and put her on the table he was supposed to occupy. He realized that this was his moment to walk into the prophecy.

He cried out, "Life, come back into her!" and she came back to life, to the amazement of all the doctors present.

Luigi's own surgery went very well that day, but he had much more to rejoice about. He was moving in a new and powerful realm of ministry, and it all started when he had given spontaneously.

There is much more power in sowing financially to someone who is operating on a higher level of glory than there is in just receiving their hands laid upon us. The reason is that we are partnering with them and serving them, so we receive the same rewards and giftings.

QUESTIONS

1. Have you ever sown into someone's glory? If so, did you do so in spontaneous obedience? Are you open to sowing into another's ministry in the future?

2. Why do you think gold dust accompanied the spirit of spontaneous giving in Montreal as stated above? Do you see God's glory in both acts? What do you think God wanted to show through these experiences?

3. In the example of Luigi above, how was God's grace transferred from the author to Luigi? How did this grace then give Luigi the anointing to raise the dead when the situation arose? Could you see yourself in his place? Why or why not?

4. What power do you see in sowing financially to someone who operates in a high level of glory? Why do most Christians resist this act of obedience and desire the person to lay hands on them instead?

5. How does sowing into a ministry of God's glory bring about a partnership? How does this concept release us to a new realm of ministry? In what way does our act of giving put us in the receiving position for rewards and giftings that the ministry operates in?

"The Bible mentions a principle called a prophet's reward (Matt. 10:42). It involves giving to a man or woman of God, as God leads, and receiving a supernatural blessing from that giving."

Who are the three or four people you most honor as having an impact in your life or in those around you?

Do they receive a prophet's reward?

Have you sown into these people in some way?

Ask God to reveal what you are to do for these people and be ready for a spontaneous unction to bless them in the future.

Day 15

Giving Releases Miracles

"Now a certain man was sick, Lazarus of Bethany, the town of Mary and her sister Martha. **It was that Mary who anointed the Lord with fragrant oil and wiped His feet with her hair, whose brother Lazarus was sick**" (John 11:1-2).

Spontaneous giving releases an atmosphere for signs and wonders and miracles and allows a person to partake of a grace working in someone else's ministry. It is a form of serving a ministry.

When Mary of Bethany broke an alabaster jar filled with expensive perfume and anointed Jesus with it, she was sowing to the Son of God. He not only had the glory; He was the Source of the glory.

To Judas, what Mary did seemed like a terrible waste. Jesus said, however, that Mary had done this "for [His] burial."

I believe that Mary had caught a revelation of who Jesus was, and as a result, she received Him as her Savior that day. She now wanted to offer something to the Savior.

The gift that Mary sowed that day was costly to her.

When we give sacrificially to the Lord as worship, it touches His heart and releases His miraculous power.

Mary had sowed to Jesus' burial and resurrection through her spontaneous and sacrificial gift, and now she would benefit from that same resurrection power. Jesus raised Lazarus from the dead.

We have noticed in all of our meetings that when this same spirit of spontaneous giving is working, the atmosphere changes, and the grace for signs, wonders and miracles is usually more prevalent.

In this acceleration of the glory, in which the Lord is taking us from glory to glory, acceleration is taking place in the area of giving also.

1. Mary's act of worship was extravagant. In what way? Mary's act of worship was controversial. How? Mary's act of worship should give us a principle of sowing into someone's ministry. What have you learned from Mary?

2. What impetus did Mary have for sowing into Jesus' ministry through her hospitality and her act of worship? What does revelation have to do with her demonstrations of love? In your opinion, what does revelation have to do with our demonstrations of giving honor to others?

3. How was Mary's gift spontaneous? What is the significance of the spontaneity of her actions? What does this tell you about how spontaneity is important to your acts of worship of God and honor of ministry leadership?

4. Mary's act of anointing Jesus was an act of humility. What part of the story shows the lowliness that was in her heart? How do our acts of sowing into others demonstrate God working humility into our character?

5. What does "acceleration of the glory" mean to you? How does God take us from glory to glory? Does God want to work acceleration in your giving? In what ways that you can see right now does He want to accelerate your giving? In what ways is God taking you from glory to glory?

MEDITATION

*"When a rich woman gave Elisha a room
to stay in, and she served him, she was sowing
into the glory on his life. She needed a son, Elisha
prophesied and the woman conceived and bore a son."*

The woman didn't have false motives
when she served Elisha. The blessing came
out of her obedience to show compassion
to the prophet. Do you have someone in
your life that God is calling you to sow
into, no matter what the outcome?

Make a plan as to how you will serve
that person in the days and weeks to come.

DAY 16

Sowing Into Good Ground Versus Sowing Into Need

"**B**UT HE WHO RECEIVED SEED ON THE GOOD GROUND IS HE WHO HEARS THE WORD AND UNDERSTANDS IT, WHO INDEED BEARS FRUIT AND PRODUCES: SOME A HUNDREDFOLD, SOME SIXTY, SOME THIRTY" (MATTHEW 13:23).

When you sow to someone who has the glory, you are definitely sowing into good ground. It is the same ground that Adam and Eve were accustomed to before the fall. The glory was in the garden, and as long as it was there, they did not have to toil and struggle to get their seed to produce a harvest because the earth of the garden was fertile and productive. Likewise, when you sow into a ministry that has the glory, you are sowing into that same good ground.

Seed sown into good ground produces a good crop: "But others fell on good ground and yielded a crop: some a hundredfold, some sixty, some thirty. He who has ears to hear, let him hear" (Matt. 13:8-9).

If you sow toward someone who is in need, that is wonderful and we must do it, but it is not the same thing as sowing into the glory. Giving to the poor or to those in need is different from sowing into the glory.

When the boy with the five loaves and two fish gave his lunch to Jesus, the Lord multiplied it to feed more than five thousand people. If the boy had attempted to give what he had directly to the poor, that would not have been wrong, but he would not have been able to feed very many poor people. Because Jesus had the glory, the food multiplied when it was given to Him. The glory is good ground.

QUESTIONS

1. Compare the concept of good ground with a ministry that has the glory. What assurances does God give us when we sow into good soil? What multiplication will we see if we sow into a ministry that has the glory?

2. What effort did Adam and Eve exert to see the harvest that Eden bore? How was this because of the glory that was present within the garden? Why do you think fertility and productivity accompany the glory?

3. What kinds of crops does God produce from a ministry that has the glory? When God asks us to sow into ministries, how difficult is it for us to trust that the crops produced will be part of God's perfect plan of glory for the earth?

4. Contrast the differences between sowing into someone who is in need and sowing into the glory. Think through differences in the donor, the channel through which the glory comes, and the recipient of the gift. What does this teach you about giving?

5. How many times have you sown directly to persons, ministries or efforts that you see have need? How many times have you sown into the glory of a ministry, not knowing what the gift would be used for? How has each instance been significant to your walk with the Lord?

MEDITATION

"The glory is good ground."

Meditate on this principle for a few minutes. Is it easy to see whether soil is good for growing or not?

Some soil is easy to identify as poor—is the same true of ministries? Some soil may look OK but need testing to see what nutrients are there—does God ask us to test some ministries out?

If God asks us to give spontaneously, how does He bypass our reason and require immediate obedience only?

Why does He do this?

Lending Versus Sowing Into the Glory

"HE WHO HAS PITY ON THE POOR LENDS TO THE LORD, AND HE WILL PAY BACK WHAT HE HAS GIVEN" (PROVERBS 19:17).

Why should we give to the ministry of a man or woman who is already financially blessed? Let us look at what the queen of Sheba did:

Now when the queen of Sheba...came to Jerusalem with a very great retinue, with camels that bore spices, very much gold, and precious stones...she gave the king one hundred and twenty talents of gold, spices in great quantity, and precious stones. There never again came such abundance of spices as the queen of Sheba gave to King Solomon (1 Kings 10:1-2a,10).

Why would anyone give such a large amount to a man who was already considered to be the richest person in the world? It was because the glory of God was on Solomon's life and kingdom. The queen of Sheba was in need of the wisdom, revelation, glory and riches Solomon had to share with her nation, and this was her way of getting it.

Her sacrifice proved to be wise. She left for home with more than she had when she arrived: "Now King Solomon gave the queen of Sheba all she desired, whatever she asked, besides what Solomon had given her according to the royal generosity" (1 Kings 10:13).

The queen of Sheba sowed into the glory and received a portion of that glory for herself and her nation. The financial blessing she received was in addition to the spiritual blessing she had received by being associated with God's people.

QUESTIONS

1. Does it seem odd to you that the Queen of Sheba brought riches when she knew that Solomon already had more wealth than he could ever use? Do you think she wanted something that wealth could buy? Do you think she brought the gifts for other reasons?

2. If you had been King Solomon, what would you have thought about the Queen's gifts? Would you have been suspicious? Would you have been flattered? What wisdom does Solomon use to receive the Queen's gifts with an open heart?

3. How did the Queen of Sheba recognize the glory that was on Solomon? Do you think she thought it was transferable? Do you think she saw it as strategic? Do you believe that the Queen valued Solomon's glory more than her riches?

4. Did the Queen of Sheba show humility when she came to Solomon's courts? In what way did she show that she recognized his importance beyond her own? Was this flattery or truly the heart of a person who wanted to bless the other?

5. Does it seem frivolous to you that the Queen didn't help poor people in her own kingdom instead of giving the treasures to Solomon? What principle do you think we should learn from her gift?

MEDITATION

"When you lend something to someone (like a pencil, for example), you usually get back only what you have lent. Giving to the poor is what you do as a result of the harvest that comes in after giving into the glory. If you gave all to the poor and got back everything you had given, you would still not be able to feed many poor people. If you sow first to ministries that have the glory, what you have sown will come back multiplied many times over. Then you have much more to give to the poor and to those in need out of your harvest."

This concept is foreign to most
of us. Meditate on it and let God
reveal its meaning to you personally.

DAY 18

Whoever Blessed Abraham Would Be Blessed

"I WILL BLESS THOSE WHO BLESS YOU, AND I WILL CURSE HIM WHO CURSES YOU; AND IN YOU ALL THE FAMILIES OF THE EARTH SHALL BE BLESSED" (GENESIS 12:3).

Abraham became the father of many nations, and God promised him great blessings. Because the blessing and glory of God was upon Abraham's life, whoever blessed him and his descendants would be blessed. This is a biblical rule.

Ministries that have the glory are surprisingly blessed on all sides. If we can stay long enough in the glory, physical needs will become less and less of a problem.

The Bible says that as long as the Earth remains, there will be seedtime and harvest time (Gen. 8:22). When we sow into the glory, we are not sowing into the earthly realm, where there is "seedtime" and "harvest." The element of time is removed or diminished in the glory. Seedtime and harvest often become the same when we sow into the glory. We reap instantly.

In Heaven there is no time as we know it. That is why, when people sow into the glory, "new money miracles" take place almost simultaneously. Money begins to multiply in the pockets, purses and wallets of the people right then and there.

Whatever God tells you to do, just do it. If He is speaking, what He is saying is coming from the glory. When you respond spontaneously to the glory, instant miracles take place. Also, since the glory is good ground, what you have given will be multiplied back to you thirty, sixty and a hundred times over. How can you lose?

QUESTIONS

1. What would it be like if you had the same blessing and glory that Abraham had? What would it feel like to bless everyone with whom you came in contact? How might the glory demonstrate itself within your family and community and church?

2. Why are "ministries that have the glory blessed on all sides"? Specifically, what does this mean? Do you think this means these ministries never have challenges?

3. Think about the earthly principle of seedtime and harvest. Have you sown prayers and petitions, gifts and service and waited for a period of time to see any sort of harvest? How do you think sowing into the glory changes seedtime and harvest? How can they simultaneously exist?

4. "Whatever God tells you to do, just do it." What does this mean? How sure must we be of God's voice speaking so that we don't ignore His voice or superimpose our own thoughts and credit their fleshly purposes to Him?

5. Does the spontaneity of our response to God's direction to sow make room for spontaneous miracles? Why? How does the principle of multiplication work?

MEDITATION

"Elijah, Elisha and Jesus all started and ended their ministries with miracles of provision. The fact that we are seeing some of the same types of miracles is a sign that we are coming into that same anointing."

Why does the miracle of provision seem so self-centered or proud to most Christians?

Is that why we have difficulty praying for and believing in it?

Is that the reason why many do not accept a word of knowledge that is given about provision?

DAY 19

A Revival of Wisdom

"FOR THE EARTH WILL BE FILLED WITH THE KNOWLEDGE OF THE GLORY OF THE LORD, AS THE WATERS COVER THE SEA" (HABAKKUK 2:14).

This verse is often misquoted. We say that the Earth will be filled with the glory of the Lord, rather than with the *knowledge* of the glory of the Lord. It is one thing to sense the glory in a meeting, and it is quite another thing to have the knowledge of that glory. When we have the knowledge, we not only sense the glory, but we have the key to releasing miracles and manifestations from that glory.

The glory could be likened to a cloud hovering over a city. The people see the cloud, but they lack the knowledge or wisdom necessary to make it rain. Clouds come and go sometimes without yielding rain. Now God is revealing to us the keys to releasing spiritual rain from the clouds of glory.

The apostle Paul knew the mysteries of revelation more than most men of his time, and this allowed him to tap into realms which other men only dreamed of. It was this gift that enabled Paul to write more than half of the New Testament. He also walked in unusual miracles, he saw the third Heaven opened, and he received multitudes of other victories.

Once you grasp a revelation of your calling in Him, then you can fully enter through its doorway with knowledge and wisdom. This is essential to walk into the frame that God has already prepared for your life.

QUESTIONS

1. Explain Habakkuk 2:14 in your own words, noting the difference between the glory of the Lord and the knowledge of the glory of the Lord. How does this revelation change the way you pursue God's glory?

2. Why do you think it is important not to just sense the presence of the glory of the Lord but also to have the keys to releasing miracles and manifestations of that glory? How can you use these keys in the future?

3. Give some examples of spiritual rain. How does spiritual rain make a difference in the life of a Christian; in the life of a community of believers; in the life of a city?

4. Think through some of Paul's revelations and mysteries that he spoke of. Do you think these were teaching tools to train him to use the keys to unlock the manifestations of the glory of God? What was his track record in terms of these manifestations?

5. "Once you grasp a revelation of your calling in Him, then you can fully enter through its doorway with knowledge and wisdom." Think through these words in terms of your own life and ministry. Are you sure of your calling? If so, what are your next steps to gain knowledge and wisdom? If not, what tools are there within your church to enable you to understand your calling in God?

MEDITATION

"Some may have wondered why at times they have sensed the glory, and yet they have never seen a physical manifestation of that glory. Having the knowledge of the glory makes the difference."

What do you know about the glory of God?

How can this knowledge be put to work for His Kingdom purposes through you?

Supernatural Wisdom
Unlocks Heaven's Supplies

"FOR WE ARE HIS WORKMANSHIP, CREATED IN CHRIST JESUS FOR GOOD WORKS, WHICH GOD PREPARED BEFOREHAND THAT WE SHOULD WALK IN THEM" (EPHESIANS 2:10).

When the same glory that is in Heaven comes down to the Earth, supernatural provision comes, and you can tap into your inheritance. Once you truly have a revelation that there is more than enough reserved for you in Heaven, you will no longer walk in lack—as long as you stay in the glory. This is why Jesus said:

> *Do not lay up for yourselves treasures on earth, where moth and rust destroy and where thieves break in and steal; but lay up for yourselves treasures in Heaven, where neither moth nor rust destroys and where thieves do not break in and steal. For where your treasure is, there your heart will be also* (Matthew 6:19-21).

If you can bring the glory of Heaven to the Earth, then the treasures of Heaven will be manifested upon the Earth. Just as gold dust has been falling from Heaven as a result of the glory, so other heavenly things can come to us.

Once we have this revelation, laying up treasure on Earth becomes a much more risky proposition. If we lay up treasure in Heaven, we can make withdrawals from it whenever we get into the glory. When we do, we will find that it has multiplied—30-, 60- and 100-fold. This is the best banking system in the world, and we don't even need an ATM card to access it.

QUESTIONS

1. "...what are the riches of the glory of His inheritance in the saints" (Eph. 1:18). How do we know that in Heaven there is no lack? What does our inheritance look like?

2. From Matthew 6:19-21 (see above), how can we be sure we are laying up treasures in Heaven and not on earth? What is the difference?

3. Why is laying up treasure on Earth risky? How does laying up treasure in Heaven bring great security? How does multiplication depend upon us laying up treasures in Heaven?

4. How can we walk in the principle of laying up treasures in Heaven on a day-to-day basis? How do you think we can walk in this revelation when we receive great blessings or when we are experiencing financial drought?

5. Do you think that the Bible tells us not to have riches? What is the difference between not seeking silver and gold for its own sake and seeking wisdom that unlocks the treasures of Heaven's storehouse of silver and gold?

MEDITATION

"When you are in need, don't just ask God to meet that specific need. Ask for wisdom, and you will know what to do to unlock more blessings. Asking God for an anointing of wisdom pleases Him and may result in a special revival of supernatural wisdom."

Asking God for wisdom can bring multiple blessings to you—what are they?

How does wisdom of the world work?

How does supernatural wisdom work?

How can you tell the difference?

DAY 21

Supernatural Wisdom Looses Miracles

" **...A**ND WHAT IS THE EXCEEDING GREATNESS OF HIS POWER TOWARD US WHO BELIEVE, ACCORDING TO THE WORKING OF HIS MIGHTY POWER..." (EPHESIANS 1:19).

TODAY'S DEVOTION

Paul prayed for wisdom for the Ephesians because he knew that this gift unlocks new realms of the glory. Another realm that wisdom unlocks is the realm of miracles. What does the phrase "according to the working of His mighty power" really mean to us? God is not only turning up the power and increasing the glory, but He is giving us the knowledge of His glory. He is teaching us the inner workings of His mighty power. He is giving us keys that will unleash the greatest miracles ever recorded.

What does wisdom have to do with miracles? Everything! Wisdom and revelation knowledge are the keys to the miracle realm. The key is simply listening to the wisdom or revelation of God and obeying it instantly—whether or not it makes sense at the time.

Jesus moved in miracle power through wisdom:

And when the Sabbath had come, He began to teach in the synagogue. And many hearing Him were astonished, saying, "Where did this Man get these things? And what wisdom is this which is given to Him, that such mighty works are performed by His hands!" (Mark 6:2)

Where did this Man get this wisdom and these mighty works? (Matthew 13:54b)

When Jesus performed miracles, people noticed that He possessed great wisdom. There has always been a direct connection between wisdom and miracles.

QUESTIONS

Use this chart to study Scriptures on the connection between supernatural wisdom and miracles.

Scripture	Key Words	Meaning	Application to Your Life
Acts 19:11-12	- Unusual miracles - By the hands of Paul - Even handker-chiefs and aprons	Paul needed a point of contact to release God's power so that he wouldn't have to lay hands on every-one that needed healing	I can pray for people via telephone, Internet, etc. and have them be just as effective as in person.
Acts 6: 8, 10	•		
Acts 7:22	•		
Daniel 1:19-24	•		
Proverbs 3:19-20	•		
Proverbs 8:22, 26, 27, 30	•		

MEDITATION

"He has made the earth by His power, He has established the world by His wisdom" (Jeremiah 10:12).

Ask God for the spirit of wisdom so that you can tap into the power of creative miracles. Then thank Him for this priceless gift with a prayer of thankfulness.

DAY 22

Supernatural Wisdom
Raises the Dead

" ...THE GOD OF OUR LORD JESUS CHRIST, THE FATHER OF GLORY, MAY GIVE TO YOU THE SPIRIT OF WISDOM AND REVELATION IN THE KNOWLEDGE OF HIM... WHICH HE WORKED IN CHRIST WHEN HE RAISED HIM FROM THE DEAD..." (EPHESIANS 1:17, 20A).

The first account of resurrection power in the Bible was found in the garden shortly after God created the Earth: "And the Lord God formed man of the dust of the ground, and breathed into his nostrils the breath [spirit] of life; and man became a living being" (Genesis 2:7).

Even though man had been formed, he needed one more ingredient—a spirit. Life is in the spirit. God then breathed a portion of Himself into man, and man lived.

I am convinced that in the days ahead the raising of the dead to life again will be one of the most common manifestations marking the last-day move of God.

When the glory comes, ask God to manifest His glory in the raising of the dead. Listen for revelation and wisdom that He may whisper into your ear. The raising of the dead is the glory of God manifested, as it was with the raising of Jesus' friend Lazarus:

> *When Jesus heard that, He said, "This sickness is not unto death, but for* **the glory of God,** *that the Son of man may be glorified through it." Jesus said to her, "Did I not say to you that if you would believe you would see* **the glory of God?"** *(John 11:4,40)*

Part of seeing the glory of God is seeing the dead among us raised to life. Jesus gave us the example, when He raised Lazarus from the dead, but we can still see these same miracles today.

QUESTIONS

1. Have you ever thought of God's creation of Adam as actually showing God's resurrection power? Explain this act in the supernatural terms that best describe it.

2. You have a portion of God within you. What is this portion usually called? How is this portion the "real you" vs. that which everyone sees as your outer physical appearance?

3. How does mouth-to-mouth resuscitation revive someone who is has no breath within them? Do you think that if unbelievers perform this successfully, then they have raised the dead? How does this physical act also need to involve the person's spirit or soul?

4. "I am convinced that in the days ahead the raising of the dead to life again will be one of the most common manifestations marking the last-day move of God." Do you believe this to be true? Why or why not? Can you see how this corresponds to the world becoming convinced that Jesus is Lord?

5. Are you open to allowing God to use you to raise the dead? Would you be able to move at a moment's notice and spontaneously breathe life into someone when God has told you to do so? If there is anything holding you back, take time to ask God to remove that obstacle.

MEDITATION

Elisha walked in this same wisdom and revelation
glory, and he also raised the dead: When Elisha
came into the house, there was the child, lying dead
on his bed. He went in therefore, shut the door
Behind the two of them, and prayed to the Lord.
*And he went up and lay on the child, **and put his***
***mouth on his mouth**, his eyes on his eyes, and his hands*
on his hands; and he stretched himself out on the child,
and the flesh of the child became warm (2 Kings 4:32-34).

Think about this truly amazing event and
what you would have seen, heard, felt and
thought if you had been an eye witness.
How does the act of the prophet lying on
the child remind you of what God did
as He created us in His image?

How does the act of putting his mouth
over the child's mouth remind you of God
breathing His life into Adam in the garden?

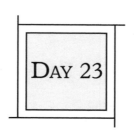

DAY 23

Supernatural Wisdom Releases Authority

"...AND SEATED HIM AT HIS RIGHT HAND IN THE HEAVENLY PLACES, FAR ABOVE ALL PRINCIPALITY AND POWER AND MIGHT AND DOMINION, AND EVERY NAME THAT IS NAMED, NOT ONLY IN THIS AGE BUT ALSO IN THAT WHICH IS TO COME. AND HE PUT ALL THINGS UNDER HIS FEET, AND GAVE HIM TO BE HEAD OVER ALL THINGS TO THE CHURCH..." (EPHESIANS 1:20B-22).

Authority comes from a supernatural revelation. God is giving us revelation concerning speaking to those in authority in any and every sphere of influence in the world. Just as the apostles and prophets of old stood before world rulers, so God is putting upon us the burden and revelation to speak to the kings and rulers of this world as a testimony before the end. As the glory increases, the favor of God will come upon many for these crucially important tasks.

Jesus walked in this authority. When He was just beginning His ministry and the men of Nazareth wanted to throw Him off of a cliff, He escaped into the crowd. They could not take Him before His time. He knew that the authority He had from His Father was greater than any authority of man.

The Bible shows us that we are seated with Christ in heavenly places (see Ephesians 2:6). Since there is no distance in the glory, we are as near to Heaven as we are to anything here on Earth. When we are in the glory, and we speak to people, we are speaking from the position where Christ has seated us in heavenly places. Therefore, people will recognize our authority. If we speak only from our position here on the Earth (without the glory), our words cannot carry the same weight. The glory represents the weight of God's authority, and kings and others in authority recognize authority when they see it.

1. Why does authority come from supernatural revelation? How do we speak on the authority of God when we operate in the glory? Are there any limits to where you might go or to whom you may speak if you continue to work within the glory?

2. "As the glory increases, the favor of God will come on many for these crucially important tasks." Have you experienced the truth of this statement? How can this be true? What is the favor of God and how do you think it is expressed on the earth?

3. Picture yourself seated with Christ in the heavenly places right now. How does this seat of authority affect the way in which you think about situations on Earth?

4. Look up the following verses and fill out the chart below:

Scripture	What I understand from this about authority	What I need to do to operate in God's authority
Matthew 10:7-8		
Philippians 1:21-22		
Acts 16:25-36		
Matthew 16:16-19		
Exodus 5:1-3		
Daniel 6:1-28		
1 Samuel 17:32-58		

MEDITATION

"In the realm of authority, everything is done by revelation and wisdom. After you receive a revelation of your seat in the heavenly places and you walk in that glory, it is no longer you speaking, but Christ in you. All authority stems from revelation in the glory, and we are experiencing a revival of that holy wisdom."

Think about how revelation and wisdom have worked in your life thus far. How does your position in glory create an entirely different view of your life?

Supernatural Wisdom Brings Favor Before Great Men

" AND THE PATRIARCHS, BECOMING ENVI-
OUS, SOLD JOSEPH INTO EGYPT. BUT
GOD WAS WITH HIM AND DELIVERED HIM OUT
OF ALL HIS TROUBLES, AND GAVE HIM FAVOR AND
WISDOM IN THE PRESENCE OF PHARAOH, KING
OF EGYPT; AND HE MADE HIM GOVERNOR OVER
EGYPT AND ALL HIS HOUSE" (ACTS 7:9-10).

God is giving us the favor and revelation to speak to any and all who are in authority so that we can reach many more people for God's glory. "You will be brought before governors and kings for My sake, as a testimony to them and to the Gentiles" (Matthew 10:18).

What do you say when God gives you an audience with a president, a banker, a judge, a police officer, a general, an actor or a warlock? You will only speak and do what you see your Father in Heaven saying and doing. Whatever comes from the throne will be backed by the authority and power of Heaven.

Some of you will speak to presidents and heads of nations and bring them a timely word from the Lord. Some will be used as Esther, to change the heart of the king in favor of the Lord's people. And some of you will be used to open entire countries to the Gospel.

Ask God for supernatural wisdom, and then do exactly as He tells you. His Word declares:

> *If any of you lacks wisdom, let him ask of God, who gives to all liberally and without reproach, and it will be given to him. But let him ask in faith, with no doubting, for he who doubts is like a wave of the sea driven and tossed by the wind* (James 1:5-6).

Make that promise yours today, and you will find your authority increasing proportionally.

1. Are you currently experiencing the favor and revelation of God? Why or why not? Do you believe that He wants you to speak to people in every strata of society, from the poor and downtrodden to those who are in authority?

2. Read Matthew 10:18 out loud, replacing the pronoun "you" with your own name. Are you prepared for this? What is the only preparation that you need?

3. Have you ever experienced God speaking through you so that the words that came out of your mouth depended not on your own intellect but came from God above? How do Christians tap into the words of the Father so that they can speak them with authority?

4. When we speak the words which God tells us, is it hard to trust that He will back up those words? Why or why not? How do you think we can keep from mixing in our own thoughts and ideas?

5. Memorize James 1:5-6. Ask liberally and receive liberally. As you gain the wisdom of the All Wise God, you are able to secure a position of authority that no earthly king could appreciate. Why is this true?

MEDITATION

*"When the Kingdom of Heaven is understood
and declared or preached, the atmosphere changes.
The revelation that the Kingdom of Heaven is here
brings in that greater glory. When you declare what God
is declaring, it begins to manifest wherever you are. Any
place can be invaded with the glory of the Kingdom of
Heaven, and every authority must bow to that Kingdom."*

What part do you play in the Kingdom of Heaven
in terms of declaring it and understanding it?

Do you see the Kingdom
of Heaven manifest wherever you go?

Do you see the Kingdom of Heaven
bringing favor upon you and making a
way of authority as you do business on earth?

DAY 25

Angelic Visitations

"ARE THEY NOT ALL MINISTERING SPIRITS SENT FORTH TO MINISTER FOR THOSE WHO WILL INHERIT SALVATION?" (HEBREWS 1:14).

Angels are used by God in many aspects of ministry—in healing, in signs and wonders, in protection, in communication, and in other ways as well. Angels are God's servants, and they carry out the orders of the King.

When the golden glory comes down, I always feel the presence of angels in our midst, and I know that Heaven is not very far away. All distance becomes relative in the glory.

Every time men or women of God have had an encounter with an angel, the experience has changed their lives. When an angel appeared to Mary, for instance, and declared that she would have a child, she was never the same again. Jacob wrestled with the Angel of the Lord, and he was never again the same. Moses' life also was completely changed after his encounter at the burning bush.

Just as in Bible days, angelic visitations today are serious experiences that often mark the opening of a new chapter in our lives and ministries. Angels deliver crucial messages from the Lord. They bring with them not only direction, but also blessings and prosperity, miracles, warnings, impartations and gifts from Heaven to minister to us.

God sends angels to help us in times of transition. Even Jesus needed the ministry of angels during His earthly ministry: "And He was there in the wilderness forty days, tempted by Satan, and was with the wild beasts; *and the angels ministered to Him*" (Mark 1:13).

1. Think about how God uses angels as His servants throughout the Bible. Use this chart to think through their ministry.

MINISTRY ACTIVITY	PERSON WHO RECEIVED MINISTRY	RESULT OF MINISTRY
Announcement of future	Mary	Became a point of hope and faith during the rest of her life
	Balaam	
	Jacob	
	Zechariah	
	Peter in prison	
	Abraham and Sarah	
	Lot in Sodom	
	Jesus in the garden	

2. How do you think God would want to use angels in these latter days? How is faith built when we have a divine encounter?

"Another of the miraculous aspects of this new move of God's glory is that we are beginning to see much more angelic activity. God is opening the heavens to His people. He is taking us into the heavens, and He is bringing the heavens down to us. Just as it has been said that the enemy, knowing that his time is short, is unleashing multitudes of demons upon the Earth, so God is releasing more angels to help us in this end-time harvest."

Have you experienced the visitation
of angels or know someone who has?

If you would receive a heavenly message
from an angel, what purpose would God
have in sending you that angelic visitor?

Why would He choose an angel
over another way to communicate to you?

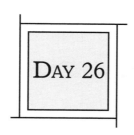

DAY 26

Revivals and Angels

"IN THESE LAY A GREAT MULTITUDE OF SICK PEOPLE, BLIND, LAME, PARALYZED, WAITING FOR THE MOVING OF THE WATER. FOR AN ANGEL WENT DOWN AT A CERTAIN TIME INTO THE POOL AND STIRRED UP THE WATER; THEN WHOEVER STEPPED IN FIRST, AFTER THE STIRRING OF THE WATER, WAS MADE WELL OF WHATEVER DISEASE HE HAD" (JOHN 5:3-4).

In every major revival, God has used angels. In Pensacola, I am convinced that a giant angel representing the holiness of the Lord facilitated many who repented and are saved. This same thing is happening in Ashland and in Toronto, as well as in Argentina.

God releases new angels to churches and ministries when He is sending them a new anointing, revival or level of ministry. These angels bring with them the new glory to be revealed. It is always the Lord's power ministering to us, but it comes through the aid of angels.

In the great healing revivals, with men such as A.A. Allen and William Branham, angels were at work behind the scenes. These men often saw them and recognized them publicly. Even in Jesus' day, angels ministered God's healing power.

God is using angels in this present move of His to show signs and wonders, to enable us to bring in the harvest.

Many times experiences such as these are considered so sacred that we keep them to ourselves and don't tell anyone for years. However, God told me to share the experiences. He showed me that time is short and that He wants more and more people to be touched in this way.

When we share an experience and declare what we have seen, that realm is opened up to those who fear, and faith is imparted to them to step into it.

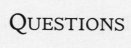

QUESTIONS

1. Did you know that in every major revival, God has used angels? Do you know of any historical revivals that had angelic visitations? Do some research on what happened in revivals of the United States and Europe. What can you learn from these historical outbreaks of God's glory?

2. Think about the angels that appeared in the New Testament. How did they minister healing power?

3. What angels are spoken of in Revelation? Skim through the book and describe their activities.

4. Why do you think people hide their experiences with angels? Do you think that they are afraid no one will believe them? Are you ready to share your sacred experiences with others so that God's witness will go forth?

5. Has anyone ever helped you overcome the fear of a new experience and brought you out of that fear into a realm of faith? Are you available and prepared to do this for someone else?

MEDITATION

"When we share an experience and declare what we have seen, that realm is opened up to those who fear, and faith is imparted to them to step into it."

Take time to pray that God will open up new avenues for His glory to be imparted to you and others. Ask Him to erase any fears or doubts you have and give you the experiences He wants you to have, including angelic visitations.

Day 27

Transported in the Spirit

"I KNOW A MAN IN CHRIST WHO FOURTEEN YEARS AGO—WHETHER IN THE BODY I DO NOT KNOW, OR WHETHER OUT OF THE BODY I DO NOT KNOW, GOD KNOWS—SUCH A ONE WAS CAUGHT UP TO THE THIRD HEAVEN. AND I KNOW SUCH A MAN—WHETHER IN THE BODY OR OUT OF THE BODY I DO NOT KNOW, GOD KNOWS—HOW HE WAS CAUGHT UP INTO PARADISE AND HEARD INEXPRESSIBLE WORDS, WHICH IT IS NOT LAWFUL FOR A MAN TO UTTER" (2 CORINTHIANS 12:2-4).

Being transported to Heaven is nothing new. Paul had this experience. This is not a new experience, yet it is new to many in our time; Heaven wants to be discovered more than we want to discover it.

We have managed to explore the far reaches of the Earth, the depths of the sea, and even planets that are billions of miles away. Man has also set foot on the moon. So Heaven is the next and final frontier.

Just as astronauts are able to bring back samples from other planets, we can bring back something from Heaven. The gold and diamonds appearing in our meetings are only the beginning of this phenomenon.

Such experiences, of course, are not unique to Christian believers. Many of those who are involved in the New Age movement have had what they call "out-of-body experiences."

Lucifer knows how things work in the spirit realm. It should not be a surprise to anyone that he has released this knowledge (in a perverted sense) to the world.

If witches are able to tap into the supernatural realm for evil purposes, how much more should we be able to discover in the supernatural how to have access to the depths of the mysteries of God's glory! He will surely release to us access to realms that no unsaved person can ever enter. It is time to accelerate in the glory realm, and many of those who are in darkness will be saved as a result.

QUESTIONS

1. Review in your mind the experience Paul had when he was transported into Heaven. Go back and read the vision in context in Second Corinthians 2. How did this experience change him?

2. If we are transported to Heaven, we can discover new things. What new things might God show us—about the Kingdom, about our lives, about the world and about the future?

3. If we are transported to Heaven, we will bring something back from Heaven. Would you tend to think that you would bring back information or revelation only? What about bringing something physical or material back from Heaven? How would this bear witness to the truth of your experience?

4. How does lucifer use spiritual experiences for his own purposes? Why do you think many in the Church have heard about these experiences first from counterfeit sources, rather than the divine true experiences from Christians?

5. How do we know that God is more powerful than lucifer? Does it stand to reason that our spiritual experiences would be more unique and powerful than any the enemy can conjure up? What brings validity to our spiritual experiences?

"Many of the people who are involved in the occult have a great hunger for the supernatural, and they have not found much in the church that can match what they have seen in the enemy's camp."

Why do you think this is true?

What kind of hunger do you
have for the supernatural?

Is hunger a key ingredient for the
church to operate in the supernatural?

DAY 28

Transported From Place to Place Here on Earth

"NOW WHEN THEY CAME UP OUT OF THE WATER, THE SPIRIT OF THE LORD CAUGHT PHILIP AWAY, SO THAT THE EUNUCH SAW HIM NO MORE; AND HE WENT ON HIS WAY REJOICING. BUT PHILIP WAS FOUND AT AZOTUS. AND PASSING THROUGH, HE PREACHED IN ALL THE CITIES TILL HE CAME TO CAESAREA" (ACTS 8:39–40).

There is no time as we know it in the glory. What takes years to accomplish on the Earth is done "in the twinkling of an eye" in Heaven's glory. That glory manifested upon the Earth will produce the same effect as it would in Heaven. Because the glory is an accelerator, God will accelerate everything upon the Earth through the glory, including travel from place to place.

Many believers have experienced being transported by the Spirit of God to some other place. Some have been transported in both body and spirit, while others have been transported only in spirit. This is an experience that God is now restoring to the Church.

There is no distance in the glory. We can pray over someone in the Spirit, and it will be as if we were there physically praying for that person. Our human spirits, when they are yielded to the Holy Spirit, can reach a person when we cannot physically be there.

There is a dimension in which we can be in two realms at the same time. In this same way, we can be in one place physically, and our spirits can be somewhere else entirely. This often happens during times of deep intercession.

In the days ahead, as we become more and more acquainted with this realm of glory, we will come to realize just how unlimited it is. Distance is nothing in the glory, and God can easily transport us from place to place.

1. Have you ever experienced your spirit being in a different place than where your body was? How does God use such an experience?

2. How does the concept of space limit our thinking to having our spirits and bodies in the same place at the same time? Since God is not bound by space, how can we experience two realms at the same time in the glory?

3. Chart out the experiences of some biblical people who were transported to other places on earth.

Person	Details That Stand Out	Application for My Life
Jesus transported during 40 days in the wilderness Matthew 4:5-6		
Ezekiel in the valley of dry bones Ezekiel 37:1		
Paul with the Colossians Colossians 2:5 1 Corinthians 5:3-5		
Elijah when the prophets were looking for him 2 Kings 2:16,17		

MEDITATION

"There is no limitation in the glory. We are made up of a body, a mind, and a spirit, and our spirits are mobile."

Why do our human minds limit the opportunities we are afforded in glory?

How can we submit our minds to the Spirit and become available for experiences that we have not yet had until now?

DAY 29

A Further Step:
Transported in Time

"SURELY HE HAS BORNE OUR GRIEFS AND CARRIED OUR SORROWS; YET WE ESTEEMED HIM STRICKEN, SMITTEN BY GOD, AND AFFLICTED. BUT HE WAS WOUNDED FOR OUR TRANSGRESSIONS, HE WAS BRUISED FOR OUR INIQUITIES; THE CHASTISEMENT FOR OUR PEACE WAS UPON HIM, AND BY HIS STRIPES WE ARE HEALED" (ISAIAH 53:4–5).

There is no time or distance in the glory. Past, present and future are all relative in Heaven. God knows the end from the beginning (see Jeremiah 1:5).

How could Isaiah claim that Jesus had already borne our sorrows, that He was bruised and wounded (all in the past tense), when Jesus had not even been born yet in human flesh? Isaiah was surely taken to a place and time in the future, and there he saw the cross. When he returned to his time, he wrote as if it had already been done. After all, he had seen it happen.

Sometimes we have dreams, and they come to pass. Other dreams don't seem to be fulfilled, but is it perhaps because we see some evil that will befall us or our loved ones or our friends, and we intercede before the Lord and prevent it from happening.

Another case of time travel occurs when the Lord shows us the future He has prepared for our lives or our ministries. It is then up to us to reach out and lay claim to it.

This is not nearly as difficult as we might think, and it certainly is not impossible. The glory that is awaiting us (future tense) in the age to come in Heaven can be brought into the present upon the Earth. We can walk into a dimension of the heavenly realm that has been prepared for our future.

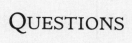

QUESTIONS

1. Have you ever experienced having your spirit in a different place from where your body was? How might God use such an experience?

2. How does the concept of time limit our thinking about the past, present, and future? Since God is not bound by time, how can we experience His perspective and experience the glory without the constraints of time?

3. Read the passage from Isaiah above. Change the tense of the words as if the events were going to happen in the future. Then read the passage as Isaiah wrote it. Do you see how Isaiah wrote these experiences as if they had already taken place? How does this expand your ideas about prophecy and fulfillment?

4. Have you ever dreamed something that eventually came true? Recall people in the Bible who received dreams that eventually came true. What does this show you about God's purposes in giving you dreams?

5. Have you ever dreamed something that became a warning? Recall some instances in the Bible where people were warned to avoid danger or negative circumstances. How did God give warnings in dreams to the prophets so that Israel could escape destruction? How might He do this through you today?

MEDITATION

*"For we are His workmanship, created in Christ Jesus for good works, **which God prepared beforehand that we should walk in them**" (Ephesians 2:10).*

"There are future events—frames—that are prepared for us to walk into. There are promises that have been spoken over our lives. The moment those promises were spoken, they were already created. They may be future, but they are just as real as anything we can touch today. As we walk into these promises, they will be actualized." God has prepared works beforehand. How did Paul gain understanding of this principle? Do you think he experienced this firsthand? How should our worldview change when we think of the past, present and future in terms of the glory?

DAY 30

Bringing Future Promises Into the Present

"... THE LAMB SLAIN FROM THE FOUN-DATION OF THE WORLD" (REVELATION 13:8B).

The Promised Land was already created and waiting for the Israelites. They only had to walk into it, and it would be theirs. Many of them failed to realize, however, that the future was already created. They were waiting for God to do something about the giants that lived in the land. The truth is that these "giants" were terrified of the children of Israel, having heard the stories of the Exodus from Egypt and of the many miracles related to their trek through the wilderness. All the Israelites had to do was obey God and walk into the land, and the battle would have been easily won. Instead, they waited another forty years, remaining in the past, and most of that generation never made it into the land.

When Jesus rose from the dead, other dead people rose from their graves and walked around the city of Jerusalem. That was a foretaste of what will happen when "the dead in Christ will rise" (1 Thess. 4:16).

Revelation speaks of "the Lamb slain from the foundation of the world" (Rev. 13:8). He was slain from the beginning of creation. When Jesus came to the Earth, it was to walk into what had already been prepared for Him.

With God, time is different. Past, present and future are not the same in His eyes as in ours. He sees them all at once and has control over them all. Time is His servant.

QUESTIONS

1. Why was it important for the Israelites to realize the fact that the Promised Land was already created and waiting for them? If they had understood this, how might that have affected their faith? How could it have changed their history?

2. Are you afraid of giants that oppose the destiny God has promised you? What lessons can you learn from the Israelites' experience that could change how you embrace these challenges?

3. How is our faith tied into the glory concept of past and future? How is obedience linked to faith? How will our spontaneous obedience be influenced if we understand the way God operates in time?

4. Did God wait for Adam and Eve to sin before He planned Jesus' crucifixion? Defend your answer. How does this fact show you that God's planning is ultimate to the destiny of mankind? What does this mean to your destiny?

5. If you were to explain to someone how God sees past, present and future, what would you say? How does this explain why God is not surprised? Even though He is control, how does this give room for our free will? How is time God's servant? How can it be ours?

*"When Jesus told Peter to catch fish, even
though he had tried all night and caught nothing,
the fish were already there waiting to be caught.
They were there from the moment Jesus had spoken
them into existence. Peter had simply to walk
into what had already been prepared."*

Has God already prepared
something for you to walk into like Peter?

Is there a miracle waiting to happen
if you just step forward and obey?

DAY 31

Delaying and Reversing Time

God can use His people to delay and even reverse time. When Jonah went to Nineveh to reveal that God was about to destroy them, they quickly repented. This reversed the time clock of judgment, and judgment was prevented—although God had told Jonah that it would surely come.

God was about to destroy the Israelites in the wilderness, but Moses saw the future and interceded for them. His faith was based on their destiny, not just their past, and through his prayers, time was reversed.

Many prophecies were given that certain cities would be destroyed because of sin. People in the churches where these prophecies were given fasted, prayed and repented for the city, and the judgment was delayed or even averted.

God can take you to a future event in the Spirit during prayer, while you are sleeping, or in broad daylight. When it happens, have faith to take that future event and turn it into a present event by declaring, prophesying, obeying and praying it into existence against all odds.

We can affect time and history. We can slow time to avert disaster or accelerate time for the sake of the harvest. It happens when we allow God to transport us to the future.

Eternity will soon replace time. As we enter into deeper realms of glory, time will seem less and less of an obstacle to the purposes of God in this generation. Let God transport you to new realms in His Spirit today.

QUESTIONS

1. Think through the story of Jonah and the Ninevites. How did the revelation Jonah gave affect the people of the city? How did the prophecy and the repentance that followed bring about a reversal of judgment? Do you think this could happen today? Through you?

2. When Moses interceded for the Israelites and averted their destruction, he saw something that even the Israelites did not see about themselves. What was it? How does intercession bridge the gap between judgment and destiny? Do you think this type of intercession takes place today? Could it happen through you?

3. How can God take you to a future event in the Spirit during prayer? Has this ever happened to you? Have you seen a future event in a dream? How could you bring this future event into the present?

4. Do you see yourself as someone who can affect time and history? Can you see the possibilities before you in the glory? Can you see time used as a tool for God's Kingdom purposes?

5. How is eternity different from time as we know it? When we enter the deeper realms of glory, why will time seem less and less of a controlling element? How can you be put in a position to experience eternity and the glory now?

"God used Joshua to reverse time for Israel. A battle was being waged, and the forces of Israel were faring well. They would need another 24 hours, however, to win the battle. Joshua acted by faith and commanded the sun to stand still in the heavens. It worked. The battle was won."

Is there a battle being waged in your life that needs "another 24 hours" of faith and prayer?

Are you willing to command the sun to stand still?

DAY 32

Miraculous Unity

"INDEED, AS I LOOKED, THE SINEWS AND THE FLESH CAME UPON THEM, AND THE SKIN COVERED THEM OVER; BUT THERE WAS NO BREATH IN THEM" (EZEKIEL 37:8).

TODAY'S DEVOTION

Through the revival of God's glory, He is bringing a unity to the Body of Christ that can only be described as miraculous. Many groups that have been separated throughout the years (because of some doctrinal difference or emphasis) are finding themselves unified in meetings where the glory is manifested. This unity is important to continued revival.

The bones of the valley of Ezekiel's vision came together when Ezekiel prophesied, and as we declare and prophesy into existence this new move of God, something is happening behind the scenes.

Before God can place the breath of life in us and cause us to experience revival and resurrection power, there has to be something substantial for Him to raise up. He does not want to resurrect just a foot, an arm, or a shoulder. Many of us are like those separated bones. We want resurrection, but what would we be if God did resurrect us? It would be strange if a hand was resurrected without the rest of the body attached to it. God could resurrect it, but even if He did, such a hand would be limited.

The next wave of revival will be of supernatural unity. It will come as God speaks and brings bones together. The bones are first shaken into place, and then God begins to form the flesh upon them.

God is sending His glory to bring the dry bones together, He will put flesh upon them, and then He will breathe life into them corporately.

1. Christians talk about unity between churches, ministries and Christians, but why do you think we can't achieve this unity in the natural? Why do you think we tend to major on doctrinal differences or our own brand of spiritual emphasis? Why does this defeat the Great Commission and the Kingdom's advance?

2. Why is unity so important to sustain revival for a longer period of time? How does the Body of Christ need to submit, both one to another and also to the overall vision of the Lord so that revival will come to us and remain?

3. Think through the dry bones vision that Ezekiel encountered. How are bones similar to the skeletal Body of Christ that we see today? What brought life to the bones? What do you think brings life to the Church today?

4. The flesh that came onto the bones that Ezekiel saw gave the bones strength, a human appearance and what else? How does this relate to the Body of Christ as the Spirit breathes flesh onto the bones of our existence?

5. "Supernatural unity" comes after the bones are shaken. What do we need to shake off so that the unity may come from above?

MEDITATION

"In the process of coming together, the bones are shaking off the dryness of the past and the pettiness that has separated believers. Then, as we see bone joined to bone, the Church is beginning to look more and more like the real Body God intended it to be."

Is there dryness within you that needs to be shaken off of your soul or spirit?

Have you ever had a petty gripe or difference with another Christian or ministry that has kept you from a relationship God has desired you to have?

Ask God to help shake off the dryness and the pettiness. Ask Him to help you hear the voice of prophecy that will put flesh on your dry bones.

DAY 33

The Breath of God

"So I prophesied as He commanded me, and breath came into them, and they lived, and stood upon their feet, an exceedingly great army" (Ezekiel 37:10).

God wants to raise up a great army, and one of the most important elements in any army is unity. The first wave of unity must be in place for the breath of life to come into a city.

Once unity is in place Jesus can give the command, and the harvest will come in. "Master, we have toiled all night and caught nothing; nevertheless at Your word I will let down the net" (Luke 5:5).

Many have toiled long and hard to get just a few fish and they now dream of a great harvest. But are our nets strong enough to hold that many fish? God wants to give us souls, but we have to be able to handle those souls once they come to us.

Once preparations are made, the catch is guaranteed:

And when they had done this, they caught a great number of fish, and their net was breaking. So they signaled to their partners in the other boat to come and help them. And they came and filled both the boats, so that they began to sink (Luke 5:6-7).

We must be mending and strengthening our nets and calling other boats to help us in the great harvest to come, for it will take all the help we can get.

We cannot do this work alone. We need many others to reap with us. We need men and women with strong nets of love and unity in the glory.

QUESTIONS

1. Why is unity so important within the ranks of an army? How does it affect the outcome of the battles that are fought? How does unity preserve the lives of the individual soldiers? Make a comparison of the importance of an army's unity to the unity that is needed within the Church.

2. Why must unity be in place before the breath of life can come into a city? What does the breath of life mean to you? Do you pray for the supernatural unity that can make your city come alive with revival?

3. Have you seen the Church work long and hard without many results for their efforts? Why is this true in so many cases? When God commands us to do the work, what do you think backs our work and creates an overflow of harvest?

4. When the disciples called out to other boats to help them, do you think that they thought about the fish the other boats may claim as their own? Do you think they were worried that they might not get credit for every fish that was caught? Why do churches and ministries look to credit and claims so often rather than to the abundance that can be for every ministry that fishes alongside of them?

5. If one local church tries to do the work alone, will revival come? Will there be experiences with the glory? Do you think that signs and wonders will be seen in abundance? How should we posture ourselves so that God can command the entire army for our city?

"Catching fish is only the beginning of the work. Afterward they must be cleaned and prepared. It is a great task. When God's great harvest begins, there will be no time for competition or jealousy. Each of us will have his hands full, as there will be much to do for the Master. Now is the time to get ready."

What kinds of things need to be cleaned from the lifestyles and souls of new Christians?

What did you have to have cleaned off of you when you accepted Christ?

What preparations should we make to not only receive the harvest but to "clean and prepare" them?

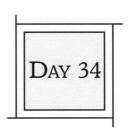

DAY 34

The Lord of the Harvest Is in Control

"THAT THEY ALL MAY BE ONE, AS YOU, FATHER, ARE IN ME, AND I IN YOU; THAT THEY ALSO MAY BE ONE IN US, THAT THE WORLD MAY BELIEVE THAT YOU SENT ME. AND THE GLORY WHICH YOU GAVE ME I HAVE GIVEN THEM, THAT THEY MAY BE ONE JUST AS WE ARE ONE: I IN THEM, AND YOU IN ME; THAT THEY MAY BE MADE PERFECT IN ONE, AND THAT THE WORLD MAY KNOW THAT YOU HAVE SENT ME, AND HAVE LOVED THEM AS YOU HAVE LOVED ME" (JOHN 17:21–23).

If we are willing, the Lord of the Harvest will cause unity to come forth. It is not our ambition, but His glory, that others must see in us.

Jesus knew that it was the glory that would make us one. The glory brings a supernatural unity that is impossible to attain with our own human efforts. In the glory of Heaven, there are no divisions, and that is what our Father wants to see among His children here on Earth.

This is the strategy we must follow. Whatever direction the Spirit shows us to go, that is always the key to victory. Sometimes it will be the time and season for the prophetic to lead the way, while at other times it will be the intercessors who will lead. Sometimes it will be time for the evangelistic gift to have its voice heard, and at other times, the Spirit will lead the pastoral giftings or some of the other gifts in the Body to become the principal voice at the moment. The Body will begin to operate as a body, with all the disparate parts working in unison.

When every part is doing its share, the fullness of God's glory will come into place, and this will cause a major growth in the harvest. Apart from the glory, our activities can be little more than man-made programs and ideas of unity. Unity is a miracle that only the Spirit can do for us.

QUESTIONS

1. Our culture has set high value on personal ambition. Yet what does God say about our ambitions? How can we show more glory and less ambition to others?

2. How does the glory make us one? Why is supernatural unity a mark of the glory?

3. How does unity reveal Heaven on Earth? How is supernatural unity a demonstration of "on Earth as it is in Heaven"?

4. What is the strategy that we must follow if we are going to see an abundant harvest? How does the Spirit + obedience ensure victory? How do you think we can know which Body part should lead at any given time? How will our submission to the Body bring further unity?

5. Have you had your fill of man-made programs and forced fleshly unity? Why is unity for unity's sake unfulfilling and a waste of time? Why do you think a miracle is needed for true unity?

MEDITATION

*"If we would learn to let the Holy Spirit lead,
we could save so much wasted time and avoid going
in the wrong direction, with the wrong people, at the
wrong time. This is important because timing is now more
critical than ever before. We must simply follow orders from
our General and Friend, trusting His prosecution of the war
effort. No war could be won if everyone did as he wished."*

How much time have you wasted because you wanted
to be in control and not let the Holy Spirit lead you?

How many times have you gone in the
wrong direction do to your stubborn will?

How many times have you had relationships with the
wrong people and it cluttered your life or set you back?

What must you do to follow orders from
the One and Only Commander of our army?

DAY 35

A Return to Our Roots

"THEN HE said to me, 'SON OF MAN, THESE BONES ARE THE WHOLE HOUSE OF ISRAEL" (EZEKIEL 37:11).

As we venture into the new, however, we cannot forget where we came from. We must rediscover our roots, if we are to possess the fullness of what has been reserved for this generation.

Ezekiel prophesied to the dry bones but these were not just any dry bones. They were "the whole house of Israel." The Jewish people have indeed been dry for the past two thousand years, but God is raising them up and giving them new life. This resurrection to new life for the Jewish people will release fresh resurrection power over the entire Body of Christ.

With Ezekiel, it took one prophecy to bring the bones together, and it took a second prophecy to breathe resurrection life into them. What would the third prophecy do? "'... and I will place you in your own land. Then you shall know that I, the Lord, have spoken it and performed it,' says the Lord" (Ezekiel 37:14).

Surely the return of the Jewish people to their homeland is an indication of the season in which we find ourselves. This was part of God's promise to the people of Israel. They would be placed in their own land, and something more: they would be resurrected from spiritual death. God promised to place His Spirit within His people after He had restored them to their land. Just as we have seen the first part of the promise fulfilled, we will also see the entire fulfillment of this promise—and soon.

QUESTIONS

1. In discovering our roots, we should look at the early church. The New Testament is full of signs and wonders, abundant harvest and outpourings of the Spirit. What made these experiences of glory wane over the years? What have we lost?

2. Did the Jewish faith have an impact on the early Christians? Did they observe traditions or did they marry their belief of Christ's salvation with the beauty of the relationship of the people of God?

3. How have the Israelites been dry for over 2,000 years? Has their rejection of Jesus resulted in a form of religion and a death to the relationship with God that His people should have?

4. Why is the land of Israel so prominent in world history? Why do you think many current world events center around this little nation? What respect should it receive?

5. How should we pray for Israel? What kind of peace do they need? Is it only a physical peace to their borders? Make Israel a point of your daily prayers.

MEDITATION

"God is about to unleash His resurrection power as we have never seen it, yet this power must be tapped into or pressed into, and this requires a concerted effort. Certain things must be contended for, as the greater glory requires a greater yearning and desire."

How easy is it for you to tap
into God's resurrection power?

How do you "press in" in
order to operate in the glory?

What kind of effort do you need to make
in order to experience God's greater glory?

DAY 36

Reconnecting to the Roots

"FOR IF THEIR BEING CAST AWAY IS THE RECONCILING OF THE WORLD, WHAT WILL THEIR ACCEPTANCE BE BUT LIFE FROM THE DEAD?" (ROMANS 11:15).

The Church was born when Jewish men and women loved the Messiah, followed Him and preached His Word to the ends of the Earth. The early Church began as all-Jewish, but was eventually composed of both Jew and Gentile. Gentiles came into the Church because Jewish believers caught a burden for the whole world.

The Church is the wild branch that was grafted in, yet we have enjoyed the benefits and become partakers of the "fatness of the olive tree":

> *For if the first fruit is holy, the lump is also holy; and if the root is holy, so are the branches. And if some of the branches were broken off, and you, being a wild olive tree, were grafted in among them, and with them became a partaker of the root and fatness of the olive tree, do not boast against the branches. But if you do boast, remember that you do not support the root, but the root supports you* (Romans 11:16-18).

Because Jesus, a Jew Himself, brought salvation to a small group of devoted Jewish men and women, salvation was made possible for all men. Our roots are in Israel, the Jewish people and the Jewish Messiah. Christianity is a branch of this root system that was formed much more than two thousand years ago.

The restoration of the Jewish people to their Messiah will bring even greater power to the world in these last days, and we will again be connected to our roots.

1. What might have happened to the spread of the Gospel if the early Jewish Christians did not preach to the Gentiles? How could we have missed out on salvation, power and glory?

2. As Gentile believers, what attitude should the Church have toward Jews who have not yet received salvation? What should our attitude of prayer be toward them?

3. Reread Romans 11:16-18. How is Israel our root? How are the Jewish people our support? Why is this important for today's Christians to understand?

4. Think back to why the Church began preaching to Gentiles in the first place. Skim through the second chapter of Acts and note the people who were present during the outpouring of the Spirit. Were there only Jews? Who else was there?

5. The decision to preach to Gentiles was a decision that caused some questions to be raised in the early Church. How did Peter and Paul settle the question? (See Acts 11.)

MEDITATION

*"Part of the purpose for God sending
this current wave of glory upon the Church
is so that we can draw the Jewish people to
their Messiah. As we do this, we will be tapping
directly into the blessing, favor and resurrection
power of God reserved for His chosen ones."*

Do you know any Jewish people?

How can you bless them with your life so
that they will trust you in the days ahead?

How will today's preparation in the natural
allow there to be openness to Jesus when
the glory comes in its next wave?

Day 37

Blessing the Jewish People Blesses Us

"I SAY THEN, HAVE THEY STUMBLED THAT THEY SHOULD FALL? CERTAINLY NOT! BUT THROUGH THEIR FALL, TO PROVOKE THEM TO JEALOUSY, SALVATION HAS COME TO THE GENTILES. NOW IF THEIR FALL IS RICHES FOR THE WORLD, AND THEIR FAILURE RICHES FOR THE GENTILES, HOW MUCH MORE THEIR FULL-NESS!" (ROMANS 11:11–12).

Today, God is leading more and more of us to bless Israel by blessing the Jewish people. We can do it through fasting and prayer and intercession, and we can do it through supporting and uniting with Messianic Jews who are witnessing to their own people. In doing this, we lose nothing. That same blessing and power that we direct toward them comes back on us.

Jews do not always understand the Gospel as we do. They must be presented with a Jewish Messiah and a Jewish faith, not necessarily with our Western ways. Our effort must not be to make them like us, but to bring them to Messiah. It is we who must return to our roots, not the other way around.

The glory of God upon the Church is the only thing that will provoke the Jewish people to jealousy today. They have known His glory better than anyone else has known it, and they will respond to its manifestation.

When the Jewish people have seen the miracles God is doing today—miracles of gold fillings and gold crowns, and the miracle of the gold dust—this has stirred them to jealousy. Signs, wonders and miracles (which are manifestations of the glory) have proven to be an effective tool in reaching the Jewish people. This is surely because it is a manifestation of the glory they once knew and for which they continually long.

QUESTIONS

1. Respect for the Jewish people and their role on the earth is the first step toward connecting with our roots. What are other steps that could be taken?

2. Do you know Messianic Jewish churches in your community? What might you do to learn more about our Jewish roots and how to love the people more? How can information aid you in your prayers for Israel?

3. How might you learn to share the Gospel to a Jew in a way that they could understand and accept? Are there people that you could talk to that could train you? Are there books you could read to help you understand what and what not to say?

4. Why is the glory of God upon the Church so important to reaching the Jewish people? How is their experience with God's glory as a people instrumental in their acceptance of the glory that would be over us?

5. The Jewish people have been longing for over four thousand years; longing for a Savior; longing for the glory of God to be manifest. How is this longing fulfilled with what we know as Christians? How can this longing help us connect with them?

*"Paul magnified and multiplied his
ministry by making the Jews jealous and
bringing them to salvation: For I speak
to you Gentiles; inasmuch as I am an
apostle to the Gentiles, I magnify my
ministry, if by any means I may provoke
to jealousy those who are my flesh and
save some of them (Romans 11:13-14).'"*

Would any Jewish people be
jealous if they looked at your life?

Do you think they would be
jealous of your church?

What do we need to be like
in order for people to desire what we have?

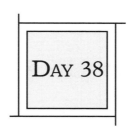

The Call to Unity

"AND THEY ALSO, IF THEY DO NOT CONTINUE IN UNBELIEF, WILL BE GRAFTED IN, FOR GOD IS ABLE TO GRAFT THEM IN AGAIN. FOR IF YOU WERE CUT OUT OF THE OLIVE TREE WHICH IS WILD BY NATURE, AND WERE GRAFTED CONTRARY TO NATURE INTO A CULTIVATED OLIVE TREE, HOW MUCH MORE WILL THESE, WHO ARE NATURAL BRANCHES, BE GRAFTED INTO THEIR OWN OLIVE TREE?" (ROMANS 11:23-24).

In this present move of God, a call is going forth to again form one Body of Christ. This Body is to be made up of both Jewish and Gentile believers.

Already Jews are being drawn to the Messiah in record numbers. Destiny is knocking at the door. We must heed the call to support the preaching of the Gospel "to the Jew first." God has promised that in the last days there would be revival in modern-day Israel (Romans 11:23-24).

God has never been unfaithful to fulfill a covenant with His people. He is a covenant-making God. We can be sure that His promises will be fulfilled, and we are nearing the time of their fulfillment.

The fulfillment of God's full promise to the Jewish people will prepare the way for His return. To get ready for that day, He is lifting the veil from our eyes so that we can see clearly to help our Jewish brethren find their way home. Jesus said to the Jews of His day: "See! Your house is left to you desolate; for I say to you, you shall see Me no more till you say, 'Blessed is He who comes in the name of the Lord!'" (Matthew 23:38-39).

The time of the fullness of the Gentiles is nearing its end, and we have a dual commission from the Lord. All nations must hear His Word before the end, and "all Israel [must] be saved" before the end. (See Romans 11:25-26.)

QUESTIONS

1. How do you think God will bring together Jews and Gentiles to form the united Body of Christ? Have you seen any signs of this happening?

2. How might churches reach out to the Jewish people and connect to their roots? How do you think this connection could become a precursor to a revival among the Jews?

3. Think through the covenant God established with the Jewish people, beginning at Abraham and going through the Old Testament. How did He always preserve a remnant even when punishing them? How did God continuously forgive them? How has this covenant been uniquely theirs?

4. How is God "lifting the veil from our eyes" so that we can see clearly and help the Jewish people? In what specific ways is He lifting the veil from your eyes? From the eyes of others you know?

5. Why is the Great Commission only fulfilled when we preach not only to the "ends of the earth," but also to Jerusalem and Samaria (the Jewish people)? What do you think it will take for the Church to seriously operate in this Great Commission in the glory?

MEDITATION

God does not want us to be ignorant of this mystery:
For I do not desire, brethren, that you should be
ignorant of this mystery, lest you should be wise in your
own opinion, that blindness in part has happened
to Israel until the fullness of the Gentiles has come in.
And so all Israel will be saved, as it is written: "The
Deliverer will come out of Zion, and He will turn away
ungodliness from Jacob; for this is My covenant with them,
when I take away their sins" (Romans 11:25-27).

A mystery is something that can only be
understood by revelation (as every other truth,
including salvation). Just as we needed a revelation
of Jesus in order to be saved, so we need a revelation
of Israel and the Church to understand the
importance of our union with every believer
for the last-day harvest. In the days to come, this
will be a key issue for the Church. Meditate on the
truths of this scripture and take time to pray for the
revelation of Jesus to come to the Jewish people.

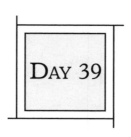

DAY 39

"One New Man"

"FOR HE HIMSELF IS OUR PEACE, WHO HAS MADE BOTH ONE, AND HAS BROKEN DOWN THE MIDDLE WALL OF SEPARATION, HAVING ABOLISHED IN HIS FLESH THE ENMITY, THAT IS, THE LAW OF COMMANDMENTS CONTAINED IN ORDINANCES, SO AS TO CREATE IN HIMSELF ONE NEW MAN FROM THE TWO, THUS MAKING PEACE, AND THAT HE MIGHT RECONCILE THEM BOTH TO GOD IN ONE BODY THROUGH THE CROSS, THEREBY PUTTING TO DEATH THE ENMITY" (EPHESIANS 2:14-16).

God is forming "one new man." God is bringing together two bodies, one Jewish and one Gentile, and making them one. The Messianic Jews have already received revelation and truth that will be beneficial to the Church, and the Church has much to offer the Jews. Our coming together will form a powerhouse for the Lord.

Many of the feasts of the Old Testament contain powerful symbolism that can unlock revelation and the power of God for us. They are prophetic and show us what is to come. This does not mean that non-Jewish believers need to look Jewish and celebrate everything exactly as Jewish believers do. It means that despite our differences we can come into oneness and a mutual understanding of the graces, revelation and truths that have been given to each of us. We are like two different shoes, and both are needed to make the pair.

Jesus said that He had not come to destroy the Law and the prophets, but to fulfill them. The wonderful presence of God's glory that comes to us when we celebrate the Communion in the Spirit is also experienced by Jewish believers when they celebrate their feasts. Jesus celebrated those same feasts, and that included the Passover meal that we have come to call the Last Supper. Both the Church and the Jews have a rich common heritage.

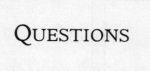

QUESTIONS

1. How does the "one new man" relate to the picture of the man and woman becoming one as they marry? How does it relate to the oneness that is within the Trinity?

2. What do you think the Jewish people have to offer the Church today? What might we learn from them that has spiritual and eternal value?

3. What do you think the Gentile Church has to offer the Jewish people today? What might they learn from us that has spiritual and eternal value?

4. When Jesus said He was going to fulfill the Law and the prophets, He brought honor to both. Why did He not just do away with them and usher a new age? Why is the New Covenant entrenched in the Old Covenant? What can we learn from this in order to not "do away" with the Jewish traditions that God established, but rather to honor them?

5. Think through the major feasts that God established with the Jewish people. What can we as a Church learn from these feasts? How is the Passover fulfilled in the Last Supper? What might be fulfilled in the other feasts (like the Feast of the Tabernacles, etc.)?

MEDITATION

"God is forming 'one new man.' God is bringing together two bodies, one Jewish and one Gentile, and making them one. This does not mean that we will be identical. Each of us is unique, and each of us has something to contribute to the whole."

Just as the parts of the Body of Christ are unique, so the Gentiles and Jews will have their uniqueness. In what ways are you "unique" to the Body of Christ?

How can your own uniqueness draw Jews and Gentiles to the Kingdom?

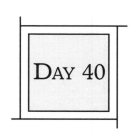

Day 40

The Time for Uniting Has Come

"For you are all sons of God through faith in Christ Jesus. For as many of you as were baptized into Christ have put on Christ. There is neither Jew nor Greek, there is neither slave nor free, there is neither male nor female; for you are all one in Christ Jesus. And if you are Christ's, then you are Abraham's seed, and heirs according to the promise" (Galatians 3:26-29).

The covenant that God made with Abraham was twofold: "In you all the families of the earth shall be blessed" (Gen. 12:3). All believers can apply this promise to bless the Earth with the Gospel. The other part of Abraham's promise is just as valid, although it was primarily for the Jewish people. It foretold that Abraham's seed would be given land as an everlasting possession.

The alienation of Gentile believers from their Jewish roots was a tragedy. It is time to heal all wounds and to receive reattachment to our roots. Let God's Spirit do the work of restoration and form the "one new man" of God's will.

The early Church began with apostles, and then there were prophets, evangelists, teachers and pastors. Now these ministries are being restored in reverse order. We have rediscovered the role of the evangelist only in the past hundred years.

Now the prophetic ministry is taking hold. The final ministry to be restored will be that of the apostle, and apostles are already recognized in some circles.

We are living in the most exciting days in all of history. We are the generation that the apostles and prophets of old longed to see. In our day, the mysteries of the glory of God are being unveiled before us, and we can look forward to the imminent fulfillment of the Lord's promise that the earth will be filled with the knowledge of the glory of the Lord as the waters cover the sea.

QUESTIONS

1. Read the two parts of the covenant that God made with Abraham in Genesis 12. Do you think one part is more important than the other? What should we do to embrace this covenant in its entirety?

2. The alienation of Jews and Gentiles has taken place over the last 2,000 years. What are some key events in history that marred the relationship? We can't erase history, but what can we learn from it?

3. Why do you think the Church began with five-fold ministry in its fullness and eventually lost its way by only seeing pastors and teachers as true ministry offices? How does the rise of evangelists and prophets signal the ushering in of a new era? Why do you think apostles are so important to the latter days on the Earth?

4. What mysteries of the glory of God have you seen unveiled during your walk with Christ? How are these mysteries "decoded"? Why do you think this is important for us as an active part of the "one new man"?

5. What is "the knowledge of the glory of the Lord"? Why is this knowledge key for our destiny on Earth? Why do you think the spread of this knowledge is to be as vast as the "waters [which] cover the sea"?

MEDITATION

"How can you be a part of this end-time harvest among God's chosen people? You can fast and pray for all Israel and for the Jewish people. You can sow into ministries that are reaching Israel and the Jewish people. And you can be a witness yourself."

Set aside time for fasting and praying for Israel and the Jewish people. Ask God to show you the ministries that He wants you to sow into so that you will be in a position to operate in the glory. Take the time to learn how to be a witness to the Jewish people.

Partner With Us

David Herzog Ministries (DHM) is totally committed to winning souls in every continent and nation of the world via large evangelistic campaigns and events, outreach evangelism teams, street evangelism, power evangelism, prophetic evangelism, music evangelism, media outreach and literature, feeding and helping the poor, training and equipping believers and via the worldwide television program, "The Glory Zone" now airing in more than 200 nations on almost every continent.

Many souls are being touched, saved, healed, and trained—so much more will be accomplished together with you.

As you have been blessed by this book spiritually, we encourage you to partner with us also financially and in prayer. Together we can make a huge difference in reaching many more souls as the time is short.

As you partner with us and sow into the glory, we believe the same glory, harvest, favor, and blessing to come on your life, family, and ministry.

We invite and welcome you to partake of this same glory and become a part of the DHM family and enter into the shared rewards and blessings of taking the Gospel with the power and love of God from Jerusalem to the ends of the earth.

To become a partner, visit us online at www.theglory zone.org.

Or write us at:

DAVID HERZOG MINISTRIES
PO Box 2070
Sedona, AZ 86339
U.S.A.

Ministry Information

Contact David Herzog and his ministry about speaking in mass harvest campaigns, conferences, revival meetings, outreaches, or to receive more information about his ministry:

E-mail: office@thegloryzone.org

Website: thegloryzone.org

Mailing Address:

David Herzog Ministries

PO Box 2070

Sedona, AZ 86339

U.S.A.

Visit the Website at: www.thegloryzone.org

If you are interested in receiving David Herzog's prayer/ partner letter, please sign up on our Website or send your name and address to:

David Herzog Ministries

PO Box 2070

Sedona, AZ 86339

Desperate for New Wine
BY DAVID HERZOG

To order a copy of this book visit our Website at
www.thegloryzone.org.

Mysteries of the Glory Unveiled——BY DAVID HERZOG

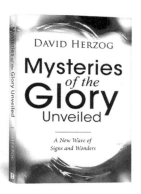

To order a copy of this book visit our Website at
www.thegloryzone.org.

Mysteries of the Glory Unveiled
Study Guide and Journal——BY DAVID HERZOG

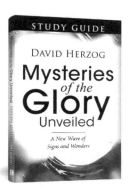

To order additional copies of this book, visit our
Website at www.thegloryzone.org.

Additional copies of this book and other book titles from DESTINY IMAGE are available at your local bookstore.

Call toll-free: 1-800-722-6774.

Send a request for a catalog to:

Destiny Image₍₎ Publishers, Inc.
P.O. Box 310
Shippensburg, PA 17257-0310

"Speaking to the Purposes of God for This Generation and for the Generations to Come."

For a complete list of our titles, visit us at www.destinyimage.com